MW00613428

SEVEN FIGURE SOCIAL SELLING

Over 400 Pages of Proven Social Selling
Scripts, Strategies, and Secrets
to Increase Sales and Make
More Money Today!

By: Brandon Bornancin

CONTENTS

ABOUT THE AUTHOR

Brandon Bornancin is a serial salesperson (sold over $100M in sales), a two-time multimillion-dollar technology entrepreneur, motivational sales speaker, and 15x sales author obsessed with helping you maximize your sales results.

Pictured above: Brandon consulting with experts like Gary Vaynerchuk, Grant Cardone, Jeffrey Gitomer, Ryan Serhant, and thousands of others.

Mr. Bornancin is currently the CEO & Founder at Seamless.AI, a software platform that delivers the world's best sales leads with the first real-time B2B sales search engine powered by artificial intelligence. Seamless.AI helps salespeople, marketers, and entrepreneurs globally find accurate emails, cell phone numbers, and pitch intelligence for any professional in the world. Seamless.AI helps over 50,000 (and counting) companies flood their calendars and generate millions in sales.

Pictured above: Brandon speaking to thousands on the art and science of building a predictable, repeatable, and scalable sales machine at Demo Day.

Mr. Bornancin is the author of over 15 sales books and the box set series famously known as *The Seven Figure Sales System*. In *The Seven Figure Sales System,* he reveals THOUSANDS of pages of proven sales scripts, strategies, and secrets that he has battle-tested throughout his career to generate over $100M in sales and build two multimillion-dollar companies. Rather than taking years or decades for you to learn these sales secrets on your own or by going through trial-and-error which is very costly to do, he's compacted everything he's learned into a sales system composed of over 15 books, training courses and his powerful list building automation platform known as Seamless.AI.

Mr. Bornancin is also the podcast host of "Sales Secrets From The Top 1%" and the author of *Sales Secrets From The Top 1%*, where he interviews the world's best sales experts on their top secrets to sales success.

Brandon Bornancin is also heavily involved in the community, helping spread awareness for whole-food, plant-powered living and for organizations supporting Alzheimer's disease, cancer, heart disease, diabetes, and many others. He lost his mother to Alzheimer's disease when he was in college and believes the food we consume can prevent the world's deadliest diseases.

He currently resides in Columbus, Ohio, and New York, New York with his wife Danielle Demming.

You can learn more about Brandon Bornancin at
http://www.brandonbornancin.com

INTRODUCTION

Throughout my sales and entrepreneurship career, I have written thousands of pages of sales scripts, strategies, and secrets that I have personally battle-tested and used to generate over $100M in sales and build two multimillion-dollar companies since I was 18.

I originally wrote this book as part of a 15-book series called "The Seven Figure Sales System" to help sales teams globally sell any product in any market to anyone by creating a predictable, repeatable, and scalable sales machine.

In fact, my team at Seamless.AI (where I am currently the founder and CEO) used these exact sales scripts, strategies, and secrets within "The Seven Figure Sales System" to grow our sales by over 1,000% within our first year of operation. These sales secrets paired with our Seamless.AI list building automation technology-empowered our team to build a multimillion-dollar business in record time in less than a year.

So instead of keeping this playbook and all the other books within "The Seven Figure Sales System" a secret, I decided to share them all with you. I want you to achieve massive sales success and I truly believe this book and all the books we write will help you get there.

And better yet - this book will work for **anyone** - no matter what you sell or who you sell to. We have worked with tens of thousands of companies across every industry and know these exact sales scripts, strategies, and secrets have proven to be successful time and time again.

But before we get into all of these sales secrets, I want to provide you with a quick background of who I am. For me, sales is not just a career - sales literally changed my family's life and I want to share that story with you to hopefully inspire and motivate you to see for yourself that sales will help you accomplish all of your biggest goals and dreams, no matter your background, education, network or upbringing.

I am also excited to share with you how I leveraged advanced sales technologies and all the sales strategies within this book to build two multimillion-dollar companies, close $100M in sales, and raise millions in venture capital funding. However, I won't just tell you my story - I'll show you the exact plug-and-play system so you can achieve this same level of success even if you have NO sales experience whatsoever. I truly believe that if you study and apply everything you learn from this book, you can generate millions in sales faster and smarter than I ever could.

FROM RAGS TO RICHES

For those of you who don't know me, I'm Brandon Bornancin, just a kid from the Midwest, out of Cleveland, Ohio.

Pictured above: My father and me at a family BBQ

I came from a lower-class family. My parents had no formal college education and were working four full-time jobs just to make ends meet.

My mother worked at a bank during the week and a grocery store at night and on the weekends. My father during the week sold computer hardware at the May Company (known as Macy's today) and spent nights and weekends working in construction.

DAVID J. BORNANCIN
MANAGER COMPUTER CENTER

THE MAY COMPANY
DOWNTOWN
158 EUCLID AVENUE, CLEVELAND, OHIO 44114
(216) 664 - 6000 EXT. 2140

Pictured above: My father's business card with the May Company

I remember when I was growing up how much my family didn't have and couldn't afford. Most of our meals were out of a can, and my mother bought all of my clothes from garage sales and the Goodwill. Back when I was a kid, I can remember getting made fun for wearing supersized t-shirts and ragged shoes. I also remember my mom spending all morning on Saturday and Sunday clipping coupons out of the newspaper to save any money she possibly could to buy groceries. Growing up, it was a tough experience, and I remember it all like it was yesterday.

My father had a different mindset than my mother. My mother always lived in scarcity and fear, while my father always dreamed big and had an expansive-like focus to do more and achieve more. Ever since I can remember, my father always worked his ass off to pay the bills and provide for our family. He had a natural-born, whatever it takes work ethic, which is why he worked two jobs in computer hardware and construction. However, his ultimate love was selling computers and he knew this type of technology would change the world for the better.

In fact, while selling computers at the May Company, he finally got his lucky break.

During one of his shifts selling computers at the retail store, a gentleman approached him wanting to learn more about a computer. After my father pitched him the computer, the gentleman was so impressed that he not only purchased the most expensive computer at the time, he also offered my father an interview for a sales analyst role for $22,000 at a high-tech computer startup called Computer Associates (CA Technologies).

The job offer was for much less than what he was currently making, but he couldn't ignore this amazing opportunity to join a tech company from the ground up. He had a hunch that a new wave of technology was coming and it would revolutionize how people worked and communicated. He thought that if he could get in early, he may have a shot at making some real money and moving up the ranks in a new technology era.

After being presented with the opportunity, my father committed to doing the interview and started studying and preparing for it day and night. When it finally came time for him to interview, he knew everything there was to know about the company, the products, and how to pitch them.

I believe my father worked so hard for weeks to prepare for that interview because he was so insecure about not having a college degree. He thought it would hold him back from ever being considered for the sales role. Back then, of course, no technology company hired anyone in sales that didn't have a college degree.

Lucky for him, this insecurity became a blessing in disguise. It pushed him to become the hardest working person in the room no matter what job he had.

My father flew out to New York for the interview and, despite having no college degree, he got the job! His weeks of preparation had paid off. After joining Computer Associates, my father continued to give everything he had. He traveled to Islandia, New York Sunday through Friday, and was rarely home the first 5-8 years of working for the company.

It was difficult for me to grow up and want to spend as much time with my father as I could. Also a blessing in disguise, it taught me early on to figure things out on my own. I was never coddled, and I had to do whatever it took to make it on my own while my father was doing the same in New York. This experience gave me the desire and determination to always do whatever it takes to be successful and provide for my family. I learned this from my father. I knew he didn't want to be away from his wife and kids every week… but it didn't matter. He always did whatever it took to provide for our family. I believe this is why I work so hard and give my all no matter what I do in life.

Pictured above: Me enjoying quality time with my father

My father quickly rose to the top of the sales pyramid over the next decade. Every 6-12 months he was promoted and went quickly from sales analyst to Account Executive, then to Sales Director and then to the coveted Vice President of Sales role, managing hundreds of top salespeople.

Throughout his decade long sales career at CA, he had accomplished massive success building the first B2B software company to ever generate over $1 billion in sales. After they generated over $1 billion in sales, he helped work with management to take the company public and it was a massive success!

Pictured above: CA went public on the Nasdaq, then NYSE. First B2B
software company to exceed $1 Billion in sales.

My father at the time was one of the highest-paid and widely
recognized V.P.'s of Sales in the industry, managing mergers,
acquisitions, and thousands of salespeople throughout his career.

During that time, I experienced first hand what it was like to go
from rags to riches, all because of sales. Throughout my father's
sales career, our lives continued to change for the better.

Every few years we moved into a bigger home, bought new luxury
cars, wore the best clothes, went to dinner at the nicest restaurants,
went on the most exotic vacations, you name it. By the time I
was halfway through high school, we lived in one of the largest

mansions in our city and I had everything I could ever dream of. I was provided for at the very highest level because my father recognized the opportunity a sales career could provide if you worked hard and gave it your all.

To this day, I can remember when my father took me to one of his big President's Club events in Hawaii. Throughout his 30+ sales career, he rarely ever missed President's Club.

When we flew in and arrived at the event, the room was filled with hundreds of the best salespeople in the world.

Pictured above: My father and other President's Club Award winners

The men were all dressed to the nines wearing expensive black and white tuxes; the women in beautiful blue and red dresses. The awards gala was like a night out at the Oscars or Grammys.

Everyone was drinking champagne, eating shrimp, steak, lobster, and all the other delicacies. I was mesmerized.

And I remember sitting there staring across the room with everyone dressed. While I was gazing across the awards gala in the sea of uber-successful salespeople, I remember my father tapping me on the shoulder telling me,

"Hey Brandon, look at all these people here all making over six and seven figures in sales..."

"Really?" I asked, in shock.

"Yep," he said.

"Look at John, he made over $1.4 million dollars this year."

"Look at Sarah, she made over $550,000."

"Jeff made over $340,000."

I was awe-struck.

Hundreds of salespeople at the event were all making $100,000, $250,000, $500,000, and many even making over $1 million in sales.

I was completely blown away.

As my dad was telling me this, I had my first big 'aha epiphany' lightbulb moment. That's when it really hit me.

All of my counselors and teachers had been telling me that if I wanted to make a lot of money, I had to become an accountant, a lawyer, or a doctor.

Yet, here I was at President's Club with hundreds of salespeople all making over six and seven figures in sales...

That was my first big epiphany, realizing I had to get into sales because if you can become a top producing salesperson, you can make any amount of money you want to make. You can become limitless, and your earning potential can become limitless too.

Right at that moment, I knew I had to get into sales no matter what it took.

Some of the people at President's Club didn't even have college degrees, and they were all making over six and seven figures in sales because success in sales is not dependent on a person's pedigree, education, background, or size of their network.

Anyone could make it in sales, as long as you put in the work. Sales is the ultimate equalizer. It's the only profession you can make the impossible possible every day.

I tell this story because my family's lives were completely transformed because of sales. It was an incredible experience to be a part of, and I cherish every second of it, both the lows and the highs throughout the journey.

Every year my father sold for CA Technologies, he won President's Club, and I remember asking him how he did it.

He always told me it was because of two things:

Build your sales list

Sell all day and night to the list.

In the early mornings and evenings, he spent all his time building prospecting lists of everyone he needed to sell to, and then during business hours, it was time to sell non-stop to the list.

From that day forward, I knew I had to go into sales.

I witnessed first-hand the importance of working hard and learning how to sell. As high school came to an end, I knew I had to go to a college that could help teach me everything I needed to learn about sales.

After looking at all the colleges nationally, I chose Ohio University because they were ranked as one of the only colleges with a sales curriculum and one of the top sales schools in the nation. It was also ranked a top business school in the state and lucky for me, also the #1 party school in the nation by an infamous magazine that ranks party schools. So I essentially got to kill three birds with one stone. Easy choice for me to make where to go to college based on the data.

When I was accepted to Ohio University, I knew I had to do two things.

First, I knew I had to find a product that I wanted to sell. My father always told me to be successful in sales, you need to find a product that you would love to sell.

Second, I knew I had to join The Sales Center at OU where I would participate in college-level sales courses, a sales training program, role-playing weekly, and required sales internships.

In the first month, I spent all of my time figuring out what the heck I should start selling.

As a big poker player, I recognized that all of my friends, family, and everyone else I knew played online poker. I was obsessed with playing online poker all day and night, and the wave of online poker was hitting the country by storm. It was everywhere on TV and college campuses. I couldn't go anywhere without a computer opened with online poker on the screen, or my buddies and I talking about how much we made or lost in online poker.

That was when the second big epiphany hit me...

I asked myself, "What if I just start selling for these online poker companies?"

So I built a list of the poker companies and started cold calling them. After a month of trying to prospect and break-in, I finally had a meeting with PartyPoker, FullTilt Poker, and PokerStars.

Pictured above: My startup poker marketing office

I pitched all three companies that I could help recruit college students to join their online poker sites. My pitch was centered around that on average, online poker companies earn $1,567 per player. I recommended they pay me $200 a player and their profits would be massive! I remember the manager at PartyPoker laughing at me hysterically because this college kid was trying to sell for them. However towards the end of the call, I was able to convince him to pay me $100 per player, and we signed the contract. Once I had that contract, I called all the other poker companies and pitched them the same deal.

Boom! Now I had a product I loved and could sell to everyone in my network.

Once I secured the product, I knew I had to start generating sales.

I started knocking dorm room to dorm room and had massive signed students up one by one. Boom, one and done.

After experiencing huge success signing up nearly everyone in my own dorm room, I went onto the next dorm and signed everyone up. Then I went onto the next building, and then the next and the next. I was generating nearly $100,000 in sales and I knew it could easily scale to millions.

However, I also recognized that knocking dorm to dorm wouldn't scale, so I started researching how to build web crawlers and scrapers.

After meeting with different engineers on campus and learning how to build a web crawler, I built my own scraper that would crawl all the OU college dorm portals that had a list of all the college students' names and emails listed. After crawling all the college dorm directories, I registered for an email marketing newsletter platform and prepared a mass blast email to them all

Not long after sending the mass emails, I signed up nearly the entire college campus that had any interest in playing online poker. After I maxed out market share at Ohio University, I knew I had to start expanding to other universities nationally. We were starting to do over seven figures in sales but to scale, I needed to get a website up and we needed to hit every college campus.

Next, I built an online website and started acquiring hundreds of customers per day, all across the nation.

Pictured above: Me in my office dorm room

The next three years in college were the best years of my life. My poker marketing company generated $1M in sales during my freshman year in college, $3M in sales during my sophomore year, and $6M in sales my junior year. It was a massive success.

Pictured above: Celebrating a big company milestone with friends

Now, I didn't get to take all that money home because we had a lot of advertising and server costs, but I can easily say I was one of the richest kids in college and had everything I ever dreamed of.

From the two-door black Mercedes hardtop convertible, four-door silver Mercedes, GSXR motorcycle, vacation house in Florida, paying off my college loans - I had everything I could ever dream of because I found a product I loved to sell, built a list and sold to that list 24/7.

Pictured above: My first two cars I bought in college paid for in cash

My life was forever changed for the better because of the list and putting in all the hard work to sell to that list.

Unfortunately, by the end of my junior year, the online poker industry started to take a downturn, and I knew the opportunity wouldn't last.

It was time to take all the money I had made, quit online poker, and launch another business.

In 2007 and 2008, text message marketing on flip phones was the newest craze, and I was ready to bet big on it.

Pictured above: My first flip phone above

My partners and I took every single penny we made from our first venture and invested it in building a mobile marketing software company called EnMobile.

We secured office space, hired 30 employees, and were on the grind day in and day out. We didn't know anything about building software. We didn't know anything about B2B sales, and we didn't know how many millions in funding we would need to develop a scalable product that could support Fortune 500 customers.

Built my 2nd company at 21, Enmobile, which lost millions due to no good B2B List

EnMobile founder and CEO Brandon Bornancin (center) stopped moving just long enough to take this photo with his staff.

Pictured above: EnMobile team, office, and awards.

Pictured above: Recognized by President of Ohio University with the coveted CEO Award (Collegiate Entrepreneurs Organization Award)

We worked our asses off for the next three years, every single day, but the venture was an epic failure. It was our first foray into B2B sales. We couldn't generate sales because we didn't know how to find the B2B sales lists to sell to. Over the course of those next three years, we lost everything we ever made from the prior poker marketing venture.

No matter how hard we worked or how much money we invested in building this mobile marketing software, we were unable to sell the product to all the B2B companies that would benefit from it. Eventually, we had to turn the lights off and shut it all down.

By this time, I had graduated from college and was completely broke. I had gone from being the richest kid on campus to bankrupt with a negative checking account balance. Sure, I was still driving my two-door Mercedes hardtop convertible that I paid cash for at 18, but that didn't really matter much since I couldn't afford to pay for the gas to drive the damn thing.

After a brutal second entrepreneurial business venture and losing everything I made, I knew I was ready to call it quits on entrepreneurship and go back to my roots and get into sales, full time.

My business partners from EnMobile went on to develop products for IBM Interactive. They pitched me to join them at IBM Interactive and start selling seven and eight-figure websites and custom software products to other marketers and IT people at IBM. I remember Jake, my former and current biz partner, calling me saying how awesome it was to build software products and websites for these massive companies and that I would love selling for them. He also mentioned not only do they have the largest brand recognition in the world but they offer free lunches most of the time. I was sold.

After trying and failing to sell EnMobile to B2B companies no one had ever heard of as just a college kid, I agreed that there wasn't a bigger and better company to sell for than IBM.

Over the next few years, I sold multimillion-dollar deals for IBM and then eventually left to sell for Google and their top search marketing agency.

Throughout my B2B sales career selling for IBM and Google, we generated a few million dollars in sales but we always struggled to be ultra-successful. Plain and simple, we were wasting all of our time in sales on endless manual list building, endless manual prospecting, endless manual CRM data entry, and endless manual appointment setting work. It had to end.

I knew that my father won the President's Club every year and built the first billion-dollar software company because he had the sales lists and always sold 24/7 to those lists.

My first company for the poker industry generated over $10 million in sales because we had the sales list and sold 24/7 to that list. My second company was a complete and utter failure because we didn't have the list. I knew when I started selling for IBM and Google to marketers and IT professionals globally, we had to get the budget to buy the lists.

So I pitched management to get the budget of $500,000 to $1,000,000 to invest in sales lists. When we finally got it, we spent nearly all of it, buying three different sales databases.

After researching social media and everywhere on the web, we knew our total addressable market was just over 500,000 marketers and decision-makers that we needed to sell to. And we knew we had to sell to as many of those people who could afford our high ticket multimillion-dollar products as quickly as possible.

When we interviewed all these sales database providers, they all told us, "Yeah, we've got all those people in our database. You just have to give us $300,000, $500,000, $100,000, etc. " depending on the database provider.

Eager to get started, we agreed and wrote the big check to each of these databases for access to their databases

The first time we ever logged in, we were dumbfounded. The databases only had a few thousand people that matched the title and company criteria that we needed to sell to. In reality, there were over 500,000 ideal decision-makers and prospective customers online.

We were missing over 90% of the people we needed to sell to. When they did have 10 out of 10,000 of the people we needed to sell to in the expensive outdated databases we just purchased, nearly 75% of the people in the database had wrong emails, wrong phone numbers, no cell phone numbers, or were no longer working at the company listed in the database. Even worse, many were deceased.

I was furious. My team was furious. And we were concerned about losing our jobs over this.

How on Earth did we just write a check for $500,000 and $1,000,000 to buy all these expensive sales databases and once we login they only have 1% of the total addressable market that we need to sell to? How do most of the contacts in this small database have bad emails and wrong phone numbers?

I knew I couldn't go back to the place I was at OU, at EnMobile, with massive office space, massive team, and a negative bank account balance, starving and losing everything I owned.

So instead of freaking out, quitting, and having to start job searching (because I knew I would get fired after I just pitched management that this massive investment in sales databases would solve all of our sales goals and dreams), I called all of my engineering friends at IBM, Google, and throughout my network. I pitched them that we have to get together to brainstorm and build something that is going to revolutionize the sales space. We got together and started whiteboarding all weekend.

Pictured above: The early Seamless team and I building the product

I remember setting the stage of the meeting by telling my friends,

"Okay, well we bought all these expensive sales databases. We're now being held hostage by these outdated sales databases because they are missing everyone that we need to sell to. And they don't have emails and phone numbers for really anyone. How do we fix this problem?"

I went on to explain, "My dad was super successful because he obsessed over the list. My first startup in online poker was super successful because we built the crawler that built the list. Our second company failed because we didn't have the B2B list that we needed to sell to so we could sell our text messaging software. Now we bought all of these lists, but they're missing all the marketers we need to sell to. What do we do?"

After whiteboarding out some ideas, I had my third biggest life epiphany big aha moment... And this one was revolutionary...

"What if IBM & Google were combined for sales?"

"Google built a search engine to find any information across the web in one search," I explained to the group.

"What if *we* built a search engine like Google did, but our own search engine to find people with the current titles working at the current companies instantly? That way we find the most updated information for everyone we need to sell to in one click?" I stated

"We could build our own real-time, people search engine!"

I knew once we had that list and could pull off actually building our own search engine, we could create our own AI technology to research emails and cell phone numbers for everyone on the list, almost like IBM did building IBM Watson that uses AI to answer any question you ask it.

If IBM Watson could use artificial intelligence to research anything in real-time, I knew we could build our own 10-step AI engine to research, validate and verify across billions of data points a B2B contact's perfect email and phone numbers.

The rest was history.

Everyone who brainstormed with me that day loved the idea, and we took it and ran with it.

From there, we started building a search engine powered by artificial intelligence that delivered the world's best sales leads and eventually is used by nearly 100,000 sales teams, marketers, and entrepreneurs to maximize sales. This search engine would be the world's first real-time search engine to find emails and phone numbers for everyone that you need to sell to.

Pictured above: The team and I working out of my house building the world's first real-time search engine to find emails and cell phones for anyone that you need to sell to.

Later, we would call our AI engine "Seamless.AI", and we would use it to research, validate, and verify perfect emails and phone numbers for anyone in the world *in real-time.*

We used our Seamless.AI prototype to generate over $100 million in sales while selling for IBM, and Google and that's when it hit me like a ton of bricks.

THE BIGGEST AHA EPIPHANY MOMENT OF MY LIFE...

MAKING OVER $100,000 in sales commissions in one month.

I remember like it was yesterday… the first time I ever made over $100,000 in one month and over $1,000,000 in one year.

It was my second year selling for Google. I landed in Vegas for a big poker conference where I was actually on PTO with my friends. It was a Friday morning, 9 am Vegas time.

I was passed out at the Cosmopolitan suite after an all-nighter poker tournament and drinking session with my friends when my accountant woke me up at the crack of dawn…

"We've got a problem," she said as I picked up the phone.

"What do you mean we have a problem?" I asked.

"If I pay you $137,000 in one month in sales commissions, taxes are going to just destroy your commission payout."

"How do you want this sliced up?" she asked.

"What do you mean, 'how do you want this sliced up'"? I mentioned.

"You meant to say a $13,000 commission check, right?" I asked, baffled.

"No," she said.

"Brandon, you were in so many back-to-back pitches and closed so many deals that we owe you $137,000 for this month's sales commissions… and that's before your salary."

At that moment, I sat back and stared at the Cosmopolitan hotel room ceiling, speechless.

My buddy Steve in the bed to the right of me looked at me saying "Are you, ok bro?"

It was right at that moment I had my next life-changing "aha" epiphany moment.

"Holy shit, I just made over six figures in sales commissions in just one month," I thought, in shock.

Right then and there I knew if I could do it using the power of Seamless and our Seven Figure Sales System, anyone in the world could do it too and I have to help them go do that right away.

I had to help others accomplish the same success that I had just achieved and I knew that instead of selling for IBM and Google making *them* millions and billions in sales, I had to help every salesperson, marketer, and entrepreneur in the world generate millions in sales with Seamless.AI, just like I did.

Using the prototype to automate all of my list building and appointment setting work was such a massive success, we had no choice but to take all the money we ever made using Seamless to go all-in on investing every penny into building Seamless from the ground up so others can accomplish the same.

ABOUT SEAMLESS.AI

Seamless.AI is the world's fastest, most accurate list building platform of all time. It's a real-time search engine powered by artificial intelligence that delivers the world's best sales leads and helps salespeople, marketers, and entrepreneurs globally automate all of their list building, prospecting, CRM data entry, and appointment setting work. This platform can be used to find emails and phone numbers for anyone in the world.

ABOUT THE SEVEN FIGURE SALES SYSTEM

As the largest power users of Seamless here at the company drinking our own champagne, having unlimited access to the Seamless.AI platform is a complete game-changer to maximize sales. We use Seamless every single day to sell and it's the number one reason we went from zero to millions in sales in record time. It's amazing to win 20-50 new customers every single day, with predictability down to the dollar and the day. However, this exciting growth also presented a massive problem for us.

Pictured above: Presenting Seamless at Demo Day in NJ!

Our calendars were flooded with 75-100 new qualified appointments every single day. My account executives were backed up in 5-10 demos each, every single day and we couldn't keep up with fulfilling the capacity.

When you have a sales team pitching every hour on the hour of every day, you need to be able to move fast, overcome any sales objection, and address any question that comes your way quickly.

That's when I realized it was time to triple down on writing thousands of scripts for every sales situation, objection and sales question my team and I would encounter. This way, we could quickly hear the question or sales objection and A/B test the best sales scripts to overcome and win those sales faster than ever before.

In sales, you are going to come across the same sales situations, questions, and objections every single day: "I'm Not Interested," "It's Too Expensive," "Already Working With Someone," "I Need To Talk To My Boss," "Send Me More Information," "Call Me Back Later," etc.

To build a multimillion-dollar software company, I knew that every person on my sales team needed to be fully prepared and trained for any sales situation and able to overcome any sales question or objection they would ever encounter.

As we built **Seamless.AI** from the ground up, we wrote *The Seven Figure Sales System* (a box set of over 15 books spanning thousands of sales scripts, strategies, and secrets anyone can use to generate millions in sales).

By using our Seven Figure Sales System and our Seamless.AI list building automation platform, our sales team was able to close millions in sales faster than ever before and build a multimillion-dollar business in less than a year. Within the first year, we also won Tech Company of the Year!

Pictured above: Our team and I winning tech company of the year

Just like we decided to stop keeping Seamless.AI our secret weapon and finally share it with the world to greatly benefit, we decided to do the same with The Seven Figure Sales System and all our books, courses, and training playbooks. We needed to share it with all of you to help you accomplish the same.

Seven Figure Social Selling, one of the 15 books within the *Seven Figure Sales System,* contains hundreds of pages of proven word-for-word sales scripts, secrets and strategies that you can use to sell any product to anyone in any market and generate millions in sales.

This book has helped us and it will help you win more sales faster than ever before.

This book is a labor of love. I know if you work hard to read it, study it, apply it, customize it, and execute selling with it, you will increase your sales, revenue and income potential.

Just remember…

You are just one list away from the life you want, the family you want, and the marriage you want. Let's build that list and help you sell to that list as fast as possible!

GOAL FOR THIS BOOK

The goal for this book is to help you generate millions throughout your sales career and become an expert at prospecting, profitable relationship building, pitching, and closing of new sales on LinkedIn and with social selling. I also want this book to help you win our Seven Figure Club Award which I highlight below.

This book will give you all of the word-for-word sales scripts, strategies, and secrets that you need to maximize your sales on LinkedIn today.

This book gives you all of your sales scripts WITHOUT having to waste your valuable time writing sales scripts for yourself AND without having to hire an expensive copywriter that costs six figures or more!

This works even if you HATE writing and never want to know ANYTHING about writing sales scripts!

Every sales script can be used immediately so you can finally avoid the awkward, poorly written sales pitches and emails, countless follow-ups with no responses back, endless selling with no success, you name it.

To maximize sales, you need to know how to sell effectively on LinkedIn. This book provides you with everything you need to maximize your success with this critical, untapped sales channel.

Becoming an expert at selling on LinkedIn is required for you to maximize your sales, income, and revenue potential. This book will provide you with everything you need to make this a reality.

This book will write all the sales scripts for you and give you all the secrets to master social selling.

This book has helped salespeople, marketers, recruiters, and entrepreneurs globally make millions in sales, get millions in funding, find partners to launch businesses, and help make business professionals dream a reality. I hope you are one of the people who work hard to use and apply all the information in this book to maximize your sales potential.

Go all-out and all-in on your success and when you do, you can win our coveted Seven Figure President's Club Award!

PLEASE WRITE A REVIEW!

If this book helps you out in any way, please help me to help others by writing a review! **http://amzn.to/2XldjAA**

Everyone is searching for books to help them improve their lives for the better... and the first thing they search for is the reviews.

If this book has a lot of amazing reviews with great comments, they buy the book and read it. If it doesn't have any positive reviews with great comments, they don't buy the book and read it.

I know this book can positively impact and help so many people... if we can get your support to write a great review with your comments on Amazon!

Additionally, I would love to read your review and hear how the book has helped you.

I print out every book review and hang them on my office wall to read for inspiration throughout the day. Your great review helps me personally to validate all the hard work and thousands of hours invested in writing this book for you.

Thank you again for reading this book and all of your support, I am truly honored and grateful.

I look forward to helping you make this next year your biggest and best yet!

YOUR JOURNEY TO PRESIDENT'S CLUB

I remember the first time I ever made over $100,000 in sales commissions in just one month and I remember the first time I made over $1,000,000 in just one year. Both of these events were life-changing for me and my family.

When it happened, I just couldn't believe it. I didn't believe it was possible for someone like me who never did great in school and who came from a blue-collar family. I knew if I could do it, you could accomplish the same and that is what I want for you this next year.

That is why I wrote this book, built Seamless.AI (The world's fastest and most accurate list building platform of all time), and most importantly, why I launched the President's Club Awards (**www.presidentsclubaward.com**)!

My goal for you this year is to win The Seven Figure Club Award pictured below on the right.

The President's Club Awards is a celebration of your sales success along this incredible journey to becoming the best that you can be in sales. We want to be there with you every step of the way, celebrating all of your major sales and achievements throughout your career.

So when you **generate over $100,000 in sales,** I will send you one of our beautiful **Six Figure Club Awards** to hang on your wall (the gold one pictured above on the left). I want you to use this as a trophy of great accomplishment, and a sign that you are well on your way to achieving something great in sales.

When you **generate over $1,000,000 in sales**, I will send you our most prized award to hang on your wall, **The Seven Figure Club Award**. This is the platinum award on the right pictured above and our most coveted award to win.

You can hang it on your wall or put it right above your computer, so when you are prospecting, pitching, and closing deals all day long, you can use it as inspiration and motivation to keep selling, keep working hard, and keep doing whatever it takes to provide for you and your family.

I want you to win this award, just like I did and hundreds of other Quota Crushers. I want your entire wall filled with these!

Some of you may be asking yourselves: "Why is getting into the Seven Figure Club so important to Brandon?"

"Why do I think it's so important for you to win?"

It's because I know the more money you make, the more people you can positively impact!

The more money you make, the more impact you can make on those around you.

Your goal, your dream, your vision, and all of your hard work this next year should be channeled into getting into this club, and it starts here inside these pages.

Maybe you're reading this, and you've already reached $100,000 or $1,000,000 in sales with Seamless.AI and our Seven Figure Sales System books, training, courses, or mastermind. If so - congratulations!

We want to print and ship you your special award so we can officially welcome you to the President's Club.

We just need you to fill out the short application via this link: **www.presidentsclubaward.com.**

If you have not closed $100,000 or $1,000,000 in sales yet, don't worry. Just keep working hard.

I BELIEVE YOU CAN DO ANYTHING.

If you're reading this book as inspiration and desperately want to get into the Seven Figure President's Club, you can sign up too!

Even though you haven't won the award yet, I'm going to help you get there.

All you have to do is join our newsletter for free at www.seamless.ai and we will send you daily tips, strategies, and best practices to get into President's Club.

Let's work hard together to make this next year your biggest and best yet.

I know you can win this award. If I can do it, so can you.

If others can do it, so can you.

Once you generate $100,000 or $1,000,000 in sales, apply for your President's Club Award here: **www.presidentsclubaward.com**

HOW TO USE THIS BOOK

The most effective way to use this book is to read it all the way through multiple times. If you already know any of the sales scripts, strategies, and secrets highlighted in this book, go ahead and skip ahead to sections or chapters that are the most important and impactful for you to increase sales today. This is your playbook to use as necessary to maximize sales. Jump to any sections most applicable to increasing your success today and go back as necessary to re-study any of the frameworks, playbooks, systems, templates, scripts, strategies, and secrets.

Please feel free to start marking, highlighting, and noting your favorite sales strategies to use right away. If something stands out to you, read it aloud several times, and identify where you can copy them and use them in your day-to-day sales efforts to maximize revenue.

This book is written as a guide for you to customize in your voice, tone, and refer to as needed. Use these sales scripts, secrets, and strategies word-for-word in your sales pitches, or as a baseline to write your own. The more you practice and refer back to these sales scripts, strategies, and secrets, the more you increase your likelihood to find and close more sales.

LEAN WRITING

I'm writing this book using a new framework I came up with called "Lean Writing." Lean writing is the act of publishing an in-progress book/ebook using lightweight tools to write fast, publish updates often, iterate in real-time, and ultimately share my sales expertise with you as quickly as possible so you can increase your sales right after reading this book.

I'm obsessed with executing lean startup methodologies and frameworks with everything I do both professionally and personally. Whether it's writing a book, launching a new revolutionary sales product or working a multimillion-dollar sales deal, I'm always striving to ship early, ship often, iterate fast from feedback and deliver the best product possible to the customer that maximizes their results.

Many people refer to this as an MVP or minimum viable product. I love launching MVPs often because it maximizes value for the customer while also providing a great opportunity to gather feedback from customers fast to iterate, optimize, and maximize results. I apply these principles to every book I write.

If I come up with an idea or strategy that could make you a million dollars but it's stuck in a Word doc or a google presentation on my computer because I wanted to wait for it to be perfectly edited, I would be holding you back from truly maximizing your sales success.

I won't ever let that happen. Publishing fast and often for the world to benefit outweighs writing for perfection. You're just one sales list, one sales script, one sales strategy, or one sales secret away from generating millions in sales. My goal is to help you generate a million dollars in sales as quickly as possible and win our coveted Seven Figure Club Award.

Reid Hoffman, the Founder of LinkedIn and the Lean Framework godfather stated in his own book, "if there aren't any typos in this book, we launched too late." Reid Hoffman is obsessed with launching fast, delivering value to the users, and gathering feedback for improvement.

I like to take the same approach as Reid to writing all of my books. Instead of taking years to write and publish a book, my goal is to gather and distribute all of the expertise and knowledge from selling millions in sales every year, building two multimillion-dollar companies, helping nearly 100,000 users with our software, interviewing the world's best sales experts on their secrets to sales success, and what I learned from our millions of readers/viewers each month engaging our social content.

My goal is to document everything I've learned throughout my lifetime and while on our journey to building a $100M company, both the successes and failures and share that information with you as fast as possible so you can quickly use these strategies to maximize your sales, income and revenue potential.

I am not a professional writer or editor. You are going to see typos, incorrect grammar, and probably many writing errors along the way when reading. That is okay, don't worry about them. The only thing that you should care about is getting as much value out of learning and using all the sales scripts, strategies, and secrets that I am sharing with you throughout the book.

Ultimately, the expectation for this book is not to please an English major or journalism school professor, but to help you and salespeople or entrepreneurs everywhere maximize their sales results FAST. I hold nothing back.

This book is being written, updated, and improved in real-time for the lifetime of its publication. If you purchased the eBook, you will get new updates as we make them in the eBook in real-time.

LEAN ACTION

As you read this book, take action and start using these sales scripts, strategies, and secrets immediately. Do not wait another second, minute, hour, day, week, month, quarter, or year. Anything you learn throughout this book can be used right away to increase your sales.

Lean action is taking immediate action and applying what you learn to improve your results throughout your sales career. I challenge you every day to take one idea or one recommendation from this book and start using them to increase your sales throughout your professional sales career.

It is said that over 97% of people who buy informational products are looking to improve their state of life but rarely do so because they never actually execute what they've learned. Please join me and the top 1% in sales by taking action and using everything you learn in this book.

It's all about finding the right sales strategies and making small habit changes while executing extensive sales activity consistently every day over long periods of time. By applying lean action sales principles, you will make all of your sales goals and income targets a reality.

Just remember… #ThereIsNoQ5 #LFG

LIFETIME UPDATES

Sales is always changing, and to accommodate the ever-changing landscape from buyers, sellers, and new technologies, I regularly update this book and that is why I decided to give you lifetime electronic updates if you purchased the eBook!

That's right, with your purchase of the eBook you get lifetime updates for free - no extra cost whatsoever. Your eBook will automatically update when changes are made or when new strategies are published!

Your success is my success, let's do this!

© 2018-2019 Brandon Bornancin

THE IMPORTANCE OF SALES SCRIPTS

Sales scripts are one of the most powerful sales tools ever created. Sales scripts are critical to master communication, persuasion, and negotiation.

All high-net-worth power players in the world have used sales scripts to get in touch and connect with anyone. You can use sales scripts to contact anyone, grow your network, win new customers, land your dream job, start a business, and even change careers entirely.

In spite of all this, no one in sales teaches anything about sales scripts or provides you with all the sales scripts needed to be successful.

Salespeople globally are very busy people and sales leaders expect that you'll somehow have the time or know-how to write hundreds of sales scripts that sell on auto-pilot.

I developed these sales scripts from over a decade of battle-tested sales experience. I write new sales scripts every day and test them throughout all of my sales efforts. This has resulted in generating over

$100M in sales, building multiple multi-million dollar companies, and raising millions in venture capital and private funding.

These sales scripts took me from being a nobody with no money and no network in Cleveland, Ohio, to launching a multimillion-dollar sales company by the time I was an 18-year-old freshman in college.

Since then, they have been improved and optimized over the years to generate over $100M in sales, raise millions in sales, secure investments from billionaire mentors, win tens of thousands of Fortune 1000 customers and connect with experts who help me maximize my own potential.

With *Seven Figure Social Selling*, you will:

- Never miss an opportunity again because you don't know what to say to the right people to connect.

- Have everything you ever need to build a world-class network.

- Consistently use and optimize scripts that convert to sales.

- Book more meetings repeatedly with the right scripts.

- Say goodbye to sounding sleazy while you sell.

- Spend time pitching and selling, without having to think about what to say and how to say it to generate sales.

The close is 20% of your selling time but 100% of your income. 100% of your income depends on closing sales and these sales scripts will ensure you can connect and close every time.

Sales is an "if this, then that" process. If this is said, then do this. If this is done, then say that. You are probably already doing this manually without even realizing it. Imagine how much more effective you can be if you begin doing it on purpose and with a plan. I guarantee you, your sales will increase.

As you read and use these scripts, I would love to hear how you personally leverage the scripts to maximize your sales success. Whether you agree with me or not, I want to hear about it. If you don't agree with me, I'd love to hear why because I know that every single actor in the world, in any movie that you've ever seen in your life, is leveraging sales scripts to deliver the best performance they possibly can. They memorize lines and they never sound like a robot. You don't have to either.

Reach out about your personal experience here,

brandon@seamlessai.com

We want to hear about your success

30 REASONS WHY YOU NEED TO USE SALES SCRIPTS

The benefits of using sales scripts to automate the sales process are limitless. If you want to sell anything to anyone in any market, you have to become an expert at writing and using sales scripts.

#1: Listen to Your Prospects

Leveraging sales scripts allows you to really listen to what your prospects are saying while you are pitching your product. If you are not using sales scripts, if you do not have a premeditated strategy or idea about what you are going to say when the prospect objects, it is a lot more difficult to get all the information you need to close the sale. Sales scripting buys you more time in each sale. You get to spend time listening instead of thinking about what you are going to say next. This gets you to the close half as fast, because you are prepared for every situation.

#2: Guide the Conversation

Scripts help guide the conversation from point A (introduction and self-discovery) to point B (pitching, closing, and winning) quickly and efficiently. They provide you with a golden path to higher conversion rates. Scripts allow you to leverage the power and experience of other top salespeople. You use exactly what is proven to bring success and strategies that are already working for top money earners in the industry. Word-for-word sales scripts close deals faster.

#3: Sell Faster

Sales scripts allow you to move faster in each sales presentation because the advanced preparation not only gives you the keys of how to handle any objection, they give you the confidence to sell powerfully and assertively. This enables you to move through as many calls, emails, social touches, and pitches as fast as possible. It's a numbers game. The more often you pitch, the more often you close. Sales scripts allow you to sell better, faster.

Objections are easy to plan for. The more prepared you are to address them ahead of time, the easier it is to close each sale.

This book is a preparation resource. It is a tool to help build your confidence so that anytime you are faced with an objection, you know exactly what to say and do next. With this book, you will never lose steam in your sale over budget issues and complaints ever again!

Top salespeople take the time before every sale to script rebuttal options for objections because they know they will run into them every single day. Objections are predictable. Your responses can be natural and effective when you use this book to practice and plan ahead. Preparing yourself with solid scripts allows you to gently handle these objections and move smoothly back into your pitch.

The sooner you put these sales scripts, strategies and secrets into practice, and the more often you refer back to them, the more effective you will become as a salesperson. Repetition is the quickest way to build progress and increase results. Your personal involvement, dedication, and implementation of the tips, strategies, scripts, and secrets inside of this book will ultimately determine how quickly you reach your own sales goals.

#4: Leverage Industry Leaders

Sales scripting lets you rinse and repeat the industry leader's top tactics and strategies. This is especially important for new sales reps. It gives you an immediate way to implement the things that really work so you can quickly ditch the extra weight of what doesn't early in your career. It eliminates the learning curve. You get to begin each sale with more confidence because you are already prepared with the most effective ways to communicate when a prospect objects to a sale.

#5: Streamline the Training Process

Sales scripts save time during the training and onboarding processes. Instead of taking 90 days to fully train a new rep, sales scripts provide you with all the tools to get them trained and fully ramped. They can become a high performing sales rep in a matter of days, maybe even in a matter of hours. Eliminate a new rep's insecurity of not knowing what to do next and you will immediately arm them with confidence that could otherwise take years of experience to build.

#6: Follow a Map

Sales Scripts are the GPS that leads you to the close. They serve as a map and navigate you to the desired destination. Scripting frees you from the worries of lost wasted time from "driving" to the wrong place. They provide a proven path, that when studied and used, leads you and the prospect to a win/win situation every time.

#7: Give the Prospect What They Want

Your prospect subconsciously expects certain things to happen at certain points during a sale. The structure of your pitch helps reveal information seamlessly and keeps the prospect hooked. Without realizing it, a well-structured pitch causes your prospect to stay engaged in the conversation and wanting more.

#8: Control the Conversation

When it comes to pitching prospects, the pacing is critical to keep your prospect interested and open to the sale. Releasing information too quickly or not allowing your prospect the time to ask questions and offer objections, takes away your power to build a personal relationship and value in the product itself. Premeditated scripts and questions give you the ability to slow down and keep control of the sales conversation.

#9: Manage the Outcome of a Pitch

Sales scripting is like movie scripting. You design the outcome. As you write and eventually edit each scene with a clear goal in mind, you will lead your prospect to the end of each scene as you direct it. Scripting gives you the director's role and allows you to write your way into a happy ending for both you and your prospect.

#10: Build a Blueprint

Homebuilders do not build before they plan. Scripting keeps you from skipping steps in your sale and allows you to get a solid blueprint in place. They give you a solid foundation and framework for your pitch so that you can find and close prospects that will turn into lifetime clients.

#11: Leverage the Power of Tonality

It's not just what you say that will make a difference in each sale, it's how you say it. Scripting and knowing your lines ahead of time allows you to maximize other aspects of communication like tonality and nonverbal communication. This keeps you from sounding nervous, or worse, like a robot. When you are calm and comfortable with your pitch and handling objections, you are able to communicate more personally. It allows you to make a real human connection so that your prospect feels like you genuinely care.

#12: Speak Efficiently

Scripts make it possible to avoid run-on sentences and paragraphs in emails or stuttering and repeating yourself over the phone and in person. They keep your pitch clear and concise which portrays confidence and experience.

#13: Avoid Sounding Like a Jacka$$

Using sales scripts keeps you from sounding like a jacka$$ when you're selling whether on the phone, virtually, or in person. It is a nightmare for a prospect to have a salesperson on the other side of the line or table who is unprepared and sloppy. Salespeople who don't use sales scripts are making calls and attending meetings unprepared. Simply put, without scripts, you are unable to share your product or service, deliver value propositions, and show all you have to offer in the most impressive and effective way possible. Sales scripts maximize the opportunity to sell and keep you from sounding like a jacka$$ who's only there to do a job.

#14: Listen and A/B Test

Sales scripts allow you to easily A/B test different variables so that you can track to see what works and what doesn't in your pitch on a day-to-day basis. By split testing and tracking your personal results, you can easily trade and use all the different variations of sales scripts to find which scripts perform better over others. This way you can constantly improve and optimize your selling efforts to maximize conversion rates. The only way to know if something works if it's tested and tracked.

#15: Leverage New Pitch Variations

Sales scripts will empower you with new ways of doing things. They give you the confidence to try something new, knowing that they have worked for others in the past. It keeps your pitch fresh and authentic. It allows you to make things interesting both for yourself and of course, your prospect.

#16: Track Your Performance

You cannot test or track your conversion rates if you do not know what you are doing and saying to get to each close. It is impossible to find what works best for you if you are not aware of what you are saying and doing and consciously testing a few different options each day. This allows you to identify whether or not a specific script and its outcome were good, bad, or neutral. This is the only way to discover exactly what is worth repeating.

#17: Track Sentiment

Choosing which scripts to use before you sit down with a client enables you to notice and track how your responses and questions make them feel and react. When you use scripts you have the time to notice and use sentiment in a sale. It gives you the ability to be more sincere. They help you gain a better understanding of how the average prospect will feel during different times of your pitch. This will help you handle emotion and the "human-ness" of each sale with greater ease and compassion. It allows for deeper connection and keeps each pitch and sale more personal.

#18: Deliver Your Best Performance

Scripts allow you to deliver the performance of a lifetime in every sale. All the best actors in the world, Robert De Niro, Julia Roberts, Matthew McConaughey, Jennifer Lawrence, and more, use and leverage scripts to deliver the best performance possible. Leonardo DiCaprio acting as Jordan Belfort in the Wolf of Wall Street delivered one of the most amazing performances of his life because of the scripts he memorized and delivered in that movie. The only way he was able to duplicate the arguably best salesman in the world, was by leveraging pre-planned scripts. He knew these scripts so well, he was able to build off of them in the moment. Scripts gave him the power to move and expand within a master plan. Does he ever sound robotic? No! There is no reason to reinvent the wheel. There is no reason to wing it. If it works for all the best actors and actresses in the world, it will work for you.

#19: Display High Emotional Intelligence

If (and when) a prospect says something that annoys you, angers you, or frustrates you, sales scripts give you the ability to maintain composure no matter the intensity of the situation. They give you a way to always display maturity, professionalism, and high emotional intelligence. You never have to worry about emotions dictating what you want to say to the prospect. This way, you stay on top of every conversation and are always able to implement a thoughtful, strategic, and positive solution-oriented response to move the deal forward.

#20: Eliminate Unnecessary Work

Sales scripting helps you eliminate non-selling work. Numerous studies by Harvard Business Review, McKinsey, Insidesales.com, Cornell University, and many others have solid research that states salespeople spend anywhere from 60% to 87% of their time on non-selling activities. The sales process is slowed significantly because salespeople are having to pause and think about how to respond during the actual process rather than streamlining it with pre-planned scripts. Communicating the best information to your prospect is time-consuming and hard work, especially if you're having a difficult conversation like overcoming sales objections. By leveraging scripts, you are able to eliminate all the non-selling activity so you can spend your valuable time using the proven word-for-word scripts to maximize your sales results.

#21: Be an Expert in Sales Instantly

Using pre-chosen sales scripts ensures you sound like an expert in your space. You will always sound confident and knowledge-able when using proven sales scripts. They allow you to focus on your speaking style and the personalization of your pitch which reinforces your expertise during the sale. It takes the guesswork out of the equation and gives your prospect peace of mind that they are working with an industry leader. Expert salespeople in every industry, leverage sales scripts so they never have to think or worry about what to say in any selling situation. You never have to sound like a first-time salesperson or an amateur selling on the phone or in person. Scripting allows you to always speak and act professionally and with authority.

#22: Ask the Right Questions

Scripts give you the ability to ask the right sales discovery questions at the right time. You will never miss an opportunity to ask a well-timed question during the sales discovery process when you leverage sales scripting. To effectively connect, identify needs, pain, and responsibilities, get to the decision-makers, define the goals, and deliver value to sell the customer. Asking the right questions at the right time is imperative. When you don't use sales scripts, you risk forgetting the most important sales questions and points required to win the deal. Missing the opportunity to ask the right question really means missing the opportunity to close a deal. Scripts will ensure you deliver the best sales discovery process possible and win more sales faster than ever before.

#23: Simplify Your Process

Sales scripts make selling simple. It streamlines the entire process. You will run into the same sales activities and the same sales challenges throughout your entire career. Make it easy on yourself!

Use what works and repeat it over and over again. Repetition is an unavoidable part of sales. It also means you can simplify how you do things. Every day you will be faced with the same questions, responses, objections, and rebuttals. Nearly every part of the process is repeated day in and day out. Rather than spending time reinventing the wheel, you can put your energy and focus on executing your pitch in a way that is proven to close more sales, faster. 95% of salespeople wing it and waste massive amounts of time as a result. Don't be one of them.

#24: Pitch at the Perfect Speed

Sales scripts allow you to pitch anyone with perfect speed, timing, and intelligence. When you are unprepared, you will feel rushed and prospects will have no idea what you are trying to communicate or accomplish. Scripts allow you to slow down so the prospect is always clear about who you are, why you are reaching out, why you want to connect with them, what your product is, and exactly what it can do for them. Scripts give you the ability to effectively communicate with the prospect at the right pace, which enables you to use the right questions and closing statements at the right time. Nerves that come from being unprepared cause salespeople to ask questions or move to close too soon. To deliver the perfect presentation, speed, timing, delivery, tone, and confidence, are essential. Scripting makes it all possible.

#25: Perfect Your Opening Statement

The opening statement of your sales scripts is the hook, line, and bait to catch your prospect's attention. Your prospect's attention is the most valuable thing they can give you during your presentation. Opening statements may be one of the most important parts of your prospecting scripts. You only have 5 to 10 seconds to catch the attention of your prospect. If your opening statement is sloppy and unthoughtful, you will have a really hard time progressing to the closing point of a sale. If it is strong, it will buy you another 20 to 60 seconds of your prospect's time. This is all you need to get in the door if you are effectively using and managing your pre-planned sales scripts. Sales scripts allow you the ability to easily test different opening statements and see which one performs the best so you can quickly maximize your sales success.

#26: Nail Your Elevator Pitch

Your elevator pitch tells your prospects who you are and what you do. You can gain them or lose them in 10 seconds. There are hundreds of ways to write and craft your elevator pitch and the only way to figure out which elevator pitch will be most successful is by testing different elevator pitches with your prospects. The elevator pitch that puts the most appointments and closes the most deals, wins. Once you have nailed it down, you should constantly reuse and optimize that same elevator pitch as one of your most important sales scripts. When you are actively practicing and using sales scripts, you are able to nail the ones that really matter. Those who take the time to do this see real and lasting results.

#27: Optimize Credibility Statements

Testing, tracking, and optimizing the performance of your credibility statements allow you to prospect and pitch more effectively and close more deals, more often. When you are prospecting and pitching, all of your scripts should include credibility statements. A credibility statement may include testimonials, case studies, and results that you delivered for a similar client. These are statements that tell the prospect how you have helped someone just like them do exactly what they needed to do in order to grow and expand their business. You will find that some companies respond to credibility statements that include testimonials more than they respond to credibility statements including case studies. The only way to write, test, track, and optimize your credibility statements, is to leverage sales scripts. Credibility statements are critical to building relevance, authority, and showcasing your experience as an expert and leader in the industry. Writing sales scripts enables you to easily identify the best credibility statements that engage and acquire new customers faster than ever before.

#28: Maximize the Call-To-Action

Your effectiveness in sales and your ability to close as many sales as possible is determined by your ability to deliver a strong, assertive, and effective call to action. This action could be asking your prospect to buy your product, asking your prospect to book an appointment, or asking your prospect to sign up for a free trial of your software. Just like your opening statements, elevator pitches, and credibility statements, the strength of your call to action at the end of each sales pitch or prospecting email, all comes down to having the best script in place. This makes the close as seamless as possible and leaves your prospect happy and wanting more.

#29: Find Your Own Voice

Reading through and practicing sales scripts allows you to find your own voice and personality during a sale. You can leverage the ideas and strategies that work, using them as an outline while you create your own and build off of them to add your individuality and personal touch.

#30: Feel Confident and Prepared

There is nothing worse than going into a sales meeting or situation feeling like you lack the necessary knowledge to move forward with the prospect effectively. Studying sales scripts gives you confidence! It allows you to walk into every sale knowing that you understand how to handle objections and keep the conversation moving towards a positive outcome no matter how many times a prospect throws them at you. Confidence is king! Your prospects can tell when you are prepared. It is impressive when a salesperson genuinely cares about their job and the service they provide to others. Sales scripts give you that edge.

SEVEN FIGURE SOCIAL SELLING

Seven Figure Social Selling is the ultimate book of Social Selling scripts giving you the world's best sales scripts to grow your connections on the largest professional network in the world. Using these scripts, you can create a repeatable, scalable and predictable step-by-step system to generate more sales on LinkedIn and crush your quota.

Get all of your Social Selling sales scripts written (in 60 seconds or less) WITHOUT spending months writing sales scripts or using sales copy that doesn't convert to sales!

This book will give you the all NEW word-for-word Social Selling sales scripts that actually writes all of your sales scripts for you!

Seven Figure Social Selling will share with you everything you need to get all your sales scripts written (in under 60 seconds) WITHOUT wasting months on writing or having to hire an expensive sales scripts copywriter!

This works even if you HATE writing and never want to know anything about writing sales scripts!

The purpose of this book is simple. I want to help you successfully generate leads, clients, and social sales.

To do this, I will share all of my Social Selling scripts that I've used after a decade of Social Selling for IBM, Google and three different startups, generating millions in sales.

These Social Sellings scripts are for you if:

- You want to generate more appointments and sales using LinkedIn.

- You know you want to grow your book of business and think LinkedIn is the network to do it.

- You have a LinkedIn profile but aren't sure how to use it as a lead generation tool.

- You've noticed that people look at your profile or connect with you.

- You don't know how to move from a LinkedIn connection to a client

- You want to acquire more customers and make this next year your biggest and best yet!

Here are some professions that will immediately benefit from the sales scripts shared in *Seven Figure Social Selling*:

- Sales Professionals and Sales Leaders
- B2B Business Owners and Entrepreneurs

- Professional Service Providers

- Coaches, Consultants, Trainers

- Speakers and Authors

- Subject Matter Experts and Emerging Thought Leaders

- Marketing Professionals

- Business Advisors

- Anyone who wants to generate leads and clients using LinkedIn!

If you belong to one of these categories, you're guaranteed to love it, to increase sales and experience more success in your career than ever before.

Like everything in life, sales is constantly changing and evolving. To respond to the changing nature of buyers, and selling itself, I regularly update the *Seven Figure Social Selling* book. When you buy now, you get 100% of the future updates for free. No extra cost whatsoever, and you'll get an email notifying you whenever updates are made.

I know you want to reach your dream buyers on LinkedIn today. Either the strategies and tactics you've used before just aren't working anymore and you're at a loss for what to do, or you're searching for a new, clear, simple easy-to-use system that you can follow to create new connections, increase brand awareness, and get more opportunities to grow your business.

What if you had a repeatable, step-by-step system that you could follow to connect with your dream buyers instantly today? Well, now you do!

THE IMPORTANCE OF SOCIAL SELLING ON LINKEDIN

With over 400 million users spreading across 200 countries, LinkedIn is the world's largest online professional network. It is the only network focused entirely on business professionals. LinkedIn connects people to each other and to opportunity. Members leverage the platform to remain connected and informed as they advance and progress in their professional careers.

The LinkedIn Mission

"Our mission is to connect the world's professionals to make them more productive and successful. We believe that prioritizing the needs of our members is the most effective and, ultimately, the most profitable means to accomplish our mission and create long-term value for all stakeholders."

The LinkedIn Vision

The vision of LinkedIn is to create an opportunity for every member of the workforce across the world. It accomplishes this by connecting individuals in the workforce to companies, job opportunities, higher education institutions, and professional knowledge. LinkedIn enables its members to create, find, and leverage professional opportunity on a global scale.

The LinkedIn Value

LinkedIn supports and enables its members to establish and manage their professional reputation through their online profile. They are able to build their professional network, research, and contact any professional on the LinkedIn platform. LinkedIn makes a massive network accessible to each of its members, no matter where they are located in the world. They create a place for professionals of any kind to stay connected and informed as they provide the ability to share relevant news, ideas, knowledge, and value. Members are able to advance in their careers by showcasing themselves and their professional skill set. Additionally, LinkedIn provides a destination for companies and corporations to attract, recruit, and hire top talent in their industry.

The LinkedIn Solution

LinkedIn ensures professionals are more productive and ultimately more successful because the platform is designed to connect talent to opportunity on a global scale. It allows for businesses and individuals to connect to each other and work smarter together.

HOW TO SET UP YOUR LINKEDIN PROFILE

LinkedIn Profile Picture

If you do not have a solid, professional profile picture on LinkedIn, you will not maximize "Seven Figure Social Selling". It is the first thing people see and will often make the difference in whether someone clicks to your page or scrolls right past. It will impact people's likelihood to respond to your messages and will determine whether or not to take you seriously in your industry field. Including a professional headshot shows commitment and respect to yourself as a working professional.

Having a strong profile photo is particularly important for sales professionals, because of your appearance online, especially if you are using the platform to set up meetings, influences how much a person trusts and values you and your opinion from the beginning. You are doing yourself a huge favor when you take the time to upload a high-quality photo.

The ideal LinkedIn profile picture size is 400 x 400 pixels. Uploading smaller files will result in cropping and viewing problems. It is okay to choose a larger picture as long as it is a square and no larger than 8MB, not exceeding 4320 pixels in height or 7680 in width.

LinkedIn Cover Photo

Similar to your profile photo, your cover photo impacts the overall feel and impression of your entire profile. Keep it clean and simple. It is also smart to include something with your company logo, the product you sell, or an image that displays what you are currently most involved in as a professional in your field. Keep it within 1584 pixels x 396 pixels for optimum viewing quality.

You may also consider choosing a photo of you on stage speaking at an event, receiving an award, or with another person of notable reputation in the industry, you are involved in. This photo can show more personality and can be used to showcase how you are unique in the sales and business world.

LinkedIn Headline

Along with your photos, your headline is the most visible section of your LinkedIn profile and is key to making a positive impression. It also helps quickly explain exactly what you bring to the table. Because it stretches across the top of your profile page, is attached to your newsfeed posts, and is displayed under your name in other users' "People You May Know" sections, it is crucial that you add something to personalize this rather than allowing LinkedIn to create one for you by default.

Your headline has a major influence on LinkedIn's search algorithm. Writing a headline that contains strategic keywords will help you appear higher in LinkedIn searches. LinkedIn shares, "If you want your LinkedIn account to be a way that people discover you or your company, you'll want to place an emphasis on keywords — words which people will search for on LinkedIn and that will show up on search engines." Your headline is the quickest way to portray yourself as a valuable key player in the sales industry.

Examples:

Sales and Sales Management Major graduating in May 2019 and looking for a full-time Sales position.

Senior Sales Executive at {{*company*}} focused on delivering {{*goal*}}.

Product Manager and Marketing Leaderin SaaSand Software within mobile, analytics, and technology space.

LinkedIn Summary

Think of your LinkedIn summary as the long form of your LinkedIn headline. This is where you add strength and personality to your profile by telling your career story. It is the easiest way to set yourself apart from the millions of other users. Leaving this section blank is a huge opportunity missed. Just like with your headline, keywords from your summary are picked up by LinkedIn's algorithm and will strengthen your searchability.

The summary section lets people know how you can help them. Leave a call to action towards the end asking people to connect and reach out to you.

LinkedIn Experience

Showcasing your professional journey on LinkedIn is how you are able to stand out to potential new connections, customers, and recruiters. In this section, it is important to include more than a list of the last five jobs you've had. Freelance work, side-hustles, volunteer time, one-on-one projects, and things beyond day-to-day work can help provide a wonderful window into who you are as a working professional and as a well-rounded, developed person.

This is especially important in sales. People will buy who you are before they buy what you sell. Your experience is what sells you to future collaborators.

Here are a few ways you can strengthen your LinkedIn experience section:

Link your job to the company you work for. This helps give context and builds credibility.

Use action words like managed, led, grew, reduced, saved, sold, etc. Tell exactly what you have done in each position. Don't just list job titles.

Use keywords. Similar to the headline and summary sections keywords still apply and boost your searchability. Research the keywords that you should include for each job or position.

Keep it clear and concise. No need to use four words when one will do. Less is more.

Go easy on the bullet points. Long bulleted lists will detract from your page.

Spotlight your achievements effectively. Instead of saying "Promoted to {{*current position*}} where I excelled in sales, increasing company revenue by 14% in my first year." Instead try, "Increased sales revenue by 14% in the first year following my promotion to {{*current position*}}." Spotlight the achievement and follow up with the title or position.

Check your spelling and grammar. Poor grammar and spelling is off-putting. It undermines you as a professional. Spend the time to make sure it's right.

Add supporting information. LinkedIn allows you to upload images, PDF's, even PowerPoint presentations. These can be used to support what you have written in your job description and may be really valuable to a person who is vetting you out online as a potential collaborator.

LinkedIn Skills

The featured skills and endorsements section is a great way to demonstrate the unique skill set you provide. Anytime someone on LinkedIn "endorses" one of your listed skills, it adds personability and credibility to your profile. This section showcases what you are qualified to do at a quick glance for anyone who visits your page. LinkedIn reported that "members with five or more skills listed are contacted or personally messaged up to 33 times more by recruiters and other LinkedIn members, and receive up to 17 times more profile views."

This is not about listing as many skills as you can. It is about listing the right skills. Below are a few of the most desired skills to have on your LinkedIn profile according to LinkedIn data:

- Persuasion

- Collaboration

- Adaptability

- Time Management

- People Management

- Analytical Reasoning

- Sales Leadership

- Creativity

MAKE MILLIONS WITH SOCIAL SELLING TIPS

Below is an extensive list of sales scripts, strategies, tips and best practices that you should always try to apply when selling on LinkedIn to maximize your sales results:

- Make it all about them, not about you.

- The more you say "you" v.s. "I" and "we", the better.

- Keep it short, ideally a few sentences max.

- Make your message interesting to your prospector connection.

- Make it mobile friendly - the majority of social media posts and messages are read on mobile now.

- Use language that's conversational, not sales-y or techy.

- The smaller the ask, the easier to answer.

- Follow up, and follow up on all of your follow-ups.

- Create a library of value-added follow-up content that you can share with your audience and connections to maximize their success. For example, we sell to salespeople so we are going to share sales strategies, tips, secrets, and best practices on anything and everything sales related.

- Make use of LinkedIn automation tools available to optimize your process.

- The more personalized the sales message, the better (i.e. name, title, company, industry, products, solutions, co-workers, customer list, blog posts, competitors, unique situation, needs, goals, solutions, market research, personas, etc).

- Write sales scripts that add value, are intriguing and unique.

- Use something relatable to discuss something complex in an interesting way.

- Leverage social proof to add credibility and build trust by mentioning to clients that they already work with. Use social proof to make people feel more comfortable and less skeptical of you.

- Make your call to action really short and simple, but also intriguing, valuable and mysterious.

- Do not use multiple call-to-actions. If you want to book a meeting, pitch booking a meeting. If you want someone to opt-in to your Freemium software, then pitch that. Not both.

- Always add value and be interesting. That way people will be excited to continue reading and motivated to respond to you, over all the other sales messages in their inbox.

- Use social proof to build trust and to help lower the perception of risk conversing with you and becoming a customer.

- Showcase relevancy by addressing something that is relevant to the target audience.

- Leverage micro-targeting and send messages to a highly targeted personalist. This hyper-targeting helps the messaging resonate with your audience i.e. VPs of sales in the computer software industry, i.e. Paid search marketers for e-commerce companies, i.e. IT managers for startups in the tech space.

- Address a specific pain point they have and offer a solution to that pain point or give a strategy/idea that can potentially help.

- Leverage the power of showing vs. telling. Show the ROI, revenue, sales results, cost savings they will get or that you delivered for a similar customer persona.

- Offer an enticing incentive for the prospects to respond to your message like an idea that could potentially help them add millions of dollars to their sales revenue. This motivates a timely response.

- Give something so valuable and attractive, while also removing anything that might create obstacles or confusion, so it is easy to say yes and hard to say no.

- Build a really targeted list that has criteria relevant to your product or service.

- The more you can address their pains, the better.

- Address a specific pain point you know they are likely to have, and then offer a potential solution to it.

- Develop credibility through social proof by demonstrating your ability to deliver results with your previous or existing customers.

- Paint a picture of what being your customer is like.

- Have a strong and clear call-to-action that incentivizes them to respond.

- Stroke your prospect's ego.

- Personalize your message and show that you did your homework. People are more likely to respond if they can tell you know something about them. (This is NOT: "Hey, I saw you on LinkedIn...")

- Be unique and original. It feels more human and will intrigue people. Treat them as your equals, not as people you worship, but still stroke their ego. (People want to connect with other interesting people!)

- Keep your call to action, short, simple and clear. Make it easy to say yes.

- Include details that are relevant to the recipient. That might include a known pain point or some recent industry news that will impact them.

- Focus on aspects of your product or company the reader will find useful. They'll be more likely to trust and engage with you when they see it's not a one-sided conversation. A good copywriting trick is to always write in the second person, as it will help both you and the reader feel like you're engaged in a two-way dialogue.

- Lure the reader in with a benefit or interesting question. For example, a line like "recapture the deal you lost" is intriguing enough to pique someone's interest but mysterious enough to make them want more. This ups the chances your email will stand out in a crowded inbox and that the recipient will open it.

- Every script should have one goal. Do not overwhelm your prospects with too many choices.

- Write mobile-friendly sales scripts.

- Read your sales scripts out loud. Reading your sales scripts aloud will dramatically improve the wording, punctuation, and phrasing of your sales scripts.

- Make your sales scripts easy to read. Space out sentences and paragraphs so it's easy to read on mobile, laptop or desktop.

- Provide clear and concise options for a prospect to easily reply with i.e. A, B or C, 1,2 or 3, etc.

LinkedIn Invite Options

There are so many ways to personalize your invitation to connect on LinkedIn using contact intelligence and company intelligence.

When reaching out to invite any prospect on LinkedIn, make sure you personalize every invite as much as possible.

If there is one thing I have learned in sales it is this; if it can be done lazily and easily, that is the way everyone is doing it.

When you send a non-personalized invitation to a prospect on LinkedIn, this makes them feel unimportant. They also immediately recognize you didn't do any research and have limited value to offer them.

I always accept a personalized invitation, especially if it shows any research was done on me or my company. If a compliment is included in the invitation to connect, I accept it even faster.

Work hard to personalize every invitation to connect with your prospects. Use data found on the contact, company, or you both.

Listed below are ways to personalize your invitation to connect on LinkedIn using contact and company intelligence found on their social networks and/or websites.

Contact Intelligence Personalization

{{*Contact*}}'s name

{{*Contact*}}'s title

{{*Contact*}}'s company

{{*Contact*}}'s headline - The short-form text area describing the member's professional profile.

{{*Contact*}}'s summary - The long-form text area describing the member's professional profile and background.

{{*Contact*}}'s previous job - The previous company the contact worked for.

{{*Contact*}}'s previous job summary - The previous company summary that the contact wrote about their previous position and what they managed or worked on.

{{*Contact*}}'s previous jobs - The previous titles and companies that the contact worked for.

{{*Contact*}}'s location

{{*Contact*}}'s industry

{{*Contact*}}'s specialties - A short-form text area describing the member's specialties.

{{*Contact*}}'s current-share - The most recent item the member has shared on LinkedIn. If the member has not shared anything, their 'status' is returned instead. If no status, this is left blank.

{{*Contact*}}'s number-connections - the number of LinkedIn connections the member has.

{{*Contact*}}'s shared connections count - The number of shared connections you have with the contact.

{{*Contact*}}'s shared connections - A list of shared connections that you have with the contact.

{{*Contact*}}'s interests - A short-form text area describing the member's interests.

{{*Contact*}}'s companies interests - A short-form text area describing the companies that the contact is interested in.

{{*Contact*}}'s groups interests - A short-form text area describing the groups that the contact is interested in.

{{*Contact*}}'s school interests - A short-form text area describing the schools that the contact is interested in.

{{*Contact*}}'s publications - Information representing the various publications associated with the member.

{{*Contact*}}'s patents - Information representing the various patents associated with the member.

{{*Contact*}}'s associations - A short-form text area listing the various associations the member is a part of.

{{*Contact*}}'s languages - An object representing the languages that the member knows.

{{*Contact*}}'s skills - An object representing the skills that the member holds.

{{*Contact*}}'s certifications - An object representing the certifications that the member holds.

{{*Contact*}}'s education - The user's educational background.

{{*Contact*}}'s courses - An object representing courses the member has taken.

{{*Contact*}}'s volunteer - An object representing the member's volunteer experience.

{{*Contact*}}'s three-past-positions - A collection of the most recent past positions that the member held, capped at three.

{{*Contact*}}'s number-recommenders - The number of recommendations that the member has.

{{*Contact*}}'s following - A collection of people, companies, and industries that the member is following.

{{*Contact*}}'s Honors-awards - An object representing the various honors and awards the member has received.

{{*Contact*}}'s member-URL-resources - An object representing the URLs the member has shared on their LinkedIn profile.

{{*Contact*}}'s Twitter Interests - The interests of the contact found from the Twitter feed.

{{*Contact*}}'s Facebook Interests - The interests of the contact found from the Contact's Facebook page

Company Intelligence Personalization

{{*Company*}} Name - The name of the company.

{{*Company*}} Type - The type of company (public company, self-employed, government agency, non-profit, self-owned, privately held, partnership.

{{*Company*}} Ticker - Company ticker identification for the stock exchange. Available only for public companies.

{{*Company*}} Website Address - The website of the company.

{{*Company*}} Industry - The industry that the company is in.

{{*Company*}} Employee Count - Number range of employees working at the company.

{{*Company*}} Specialties - What the company specializes in.

{{*Company*}} Location - The location of the company.

{{*Company*}} Logo - The logo of the company.

{{*Company*}} Blog - The blog of the company.

{{*Company*}} Blog post - A blog post written by someone within the company.

{{*Company*}} Twitter - The Twitter handle of the company.

{{*Company*}} Twitter Post - A Twitter post made on the company Twitter handle.

{{*Company*}} Description - The long-form company description, up to 500 characters.

{{*Company*}} Founded Year - The year listed for the company's founding.

{{*Company*}} Followers - The number of followers for the company profile.

{{*Company*}} City - The city that the company is located.

{{*Company*}} State - The state that the company is located in.

{{*Company*}} Products - The products that the company sells.

{{*Company*}} Competitors - The competitors of the company.

{{*Company*}} Headline - The headline of the company.

{{*Company*}} Industry - The industry of the company.

{{*Company*}} Location - The location of the company.

{{*Company*}} Employee Count Exact - The exact number of employees listed on LinkedIn.

{{*Company*}} News - News about the company.

{{*Company*}} LinkedIn Post - A post from the company on the LinkedIn Company Page.

{{*Company*}} 1st Degree Connections - A list of all the 1st-degree connections that you have with someone at the company.

{{*Company*}} 2nd Degree Connections - A list of all the 2nd-degree connections that you have working at the company.

{{*Company*}} 3rd Degree Connections - A list of all the 3rd-degree connections that you have working at the company.

{{*Company*}} Funding Rounds - The rounds of funding and amount of funding raised by the company.

{{*Company*}} Investors - A list of investors who have invested in the company.

{{*Company*}} Acquisitions - A list of acquisitions that the company has made.

{{*Company*}} Stock Performance - The performance of the company stock.

{{*Company*}} Web Technologies - The list of web technologies a company is using.

{{*Company*}} Web Traffic Data - Data on how the company website is performing.

{{*Company*}} Patents & Trademarks - A list of patents and trademarks that the company has.

{{*Company*}} Current Employees - A list of current employees at the company.

{{*Company*}} Past Employees - A list of employees that worked for the company in the past.

{{*Company*}} Events - A list of events that the company sponsored, exhibited, hosted or attended.

{{*Company*}} Stock Price - The current stock price of the company.

HOW TO WRITE THE PERFECT LINKEDIN MESSAGE

6 Steps to Writing the Perfect LI Message

As the CEO and founder of **Seamless.AI**, I get hundreds and hundreds of cold LinkedIn messages. I am the CEO and founder of a small SaaS tech startup, not of a massive tech company and still, 98% of the time someone connects with me, they send me a cold LinkedIn message pitching me their product.

Every single one of these messages, no matter how long, pitch a productor service effectively and are often off-putting.

For example:

"Hi Brandon, this is John at Marketo. Marketo is a full-service marketing automation software solution that provides omnichannel marketing at scale. We will allow you to manage all of your digital marketing channels smarter and easier than ever before so that you have the power of using digital marketing to maximize impressions, increase conversion rates, and lift up sales leads. Marketo has been in business since 2019, and we have worked with 1,000 Fortune 500 companies, like Amazon, Adobe, IBM, Dell. We also recently won an award for being the best marketing automation solution by Gardner. I would love to set up an hour-long call to meet with you and share more the power of Marketo marketing automation solutions. Thank you. Let me know. Please click my calendar, review my calendar, and book a time with me so that I can get a meeting on my calendar and fill you in my pipeline, and tell my manager that I've booked an appointment. Thanks, John."

I get this kind of cold LinkedIn message every single day and am left amazed at the amount of cold, non-researched, sales-y, uncaring messages that flood my inbox. The senders have obviously spent no time looking into who I am or what I do. They have not tried to understand the current status of **Seamless.AI** or where it needs to go tomorrow. They offer no personalization or real solution for how they can help me. Why would I respond to a message like that?

The real issue is, we all send messages like this and most of the time they fall flat. For this reason, I decided to piece together the anatomy of an effective cold LinkedIn message, so that we can all be more effective with our time and more intentional with our approach.

This kind of message consists of six steps. These six steps allow you to master cold LinkedIn messages that ultimately result in booked appointments. The acronym to help you remember these steps is, RCVSIC.

1. Research

Research the contact and company before you send any message on LinkedIn. Failing to do this makes you look and sound like you are stuck in 1980 with the Yellow Book. It is not 1980. You can research the contact and company before you send a LinkedIn message in two seconds using **Seamless.AI**, LinkedIn, Google, and a number of other resources all instantly available. Go online, to any platform and type in the company or the contact. You will find thousands of data points that will allow you to send a message worth responding to.

The beauty of being alive and selling today is that we are in a digital sharing economy. Everyone is online, everyone is sharing everything, and they are being super loud about what they are sharing. It is easy to find the information you need to write a compelling, personal cold message.

Research the contact or company before you send a LinkedIn message so that you have the information you need about them in order to communicate in a way that benefits both of you. The focus of these messages must be on where the contact's company is today, where they need to go tomorrow, and how you can help them.

2. Compliment

Compliment the contact or company within the first sentence. When you do your research, it is easy to find the amazing things these companies and contacts are doing in their field. These people are changing the world of sales, marketing, IT, HR, communications, decision-making, business development, and people forever. Every company and every contact in the world has something special about them. Figure out what that is and let them know you noticed.

Figure out what you value and admire about the company or contact, and tell them within the first sentence of your message on LinkedIn. It is a great way to show that you have done your research and care about what they are doing in the world around them.

3. Value Proposition

Deliver a compelling, life-changing value proposition statement. The structure looks like this, "We help X do Y without W or Z".

$$X = Persona$$

$$Y = Desired\ Result$$

$$W = Pain\ 1$$

$$Z = Pain\ 2$$

Pick one persona. Pick one title. Don't pick twelve titles, pick one. "We help X do Y." You have to answer the question, what is the one biggest desired result that your Y (your prospect) is dying for?

What is that biggest desired result (Y), that you, (X) can deliver to your prospect?

Write so your prospect understands you help one title do one result, without the pain of W or Z.

When you say,

"Hi, John. I love the work that you're doing over at Marketo. Congratulations on being acquired by Vista Equity. I heard that you guys are focused on massive growth because I saw that Vista

Equity and your management team was hiring 400 new salespeople. Congratulations.", you've shown that you have done your research and you have complimented them.

Next, deliver a compelling, life-changing value proposition statement:

"I'm reaching out because we help digital marketers acquire new B2B customers without increasing the cost per acquisition or the media budget."

"We help X do Y without W or Z." It's critical to nail that.

4. Social proof and credibility

Any message you send must show social proof and credibility. It is your job to make your prospect want to listen to you.

Once you have caught their attention with "We help X do Y without W or Z" the next thing that happens in their mind is this series of questions,

"Should I trust this company?"
"Who the h*ll is this person cold messaging me on LinkedIn?"
"Why should I trust them?"
"Who are they?"
"Should I believe a word that they say?"

Your social proof and credibility builds trust and respect. When providing social proof and building credibility, leverage these four key pillars:

- Logos

- Case studies

- Success stories

- Testimonial

When you deliver a solid "We help X do Y without W or Z" statement, followed by strong social proof and credibility with logos, case studies, success stories, and testimonials. You'll have them hooked.

5. Introduction

Your introduction can include simple statements like, "Hi it's {{*name*}} with {{*company*}}, I'd love to show you…" "I'd love to share strategies…"

"I'd love to share tips…" "I'd love to share secrets…"

"I'd love to walk you through how we can potentially help you accomplish the same over a quick five minute chat."

Keep this short and sweet.

6. Call to Action

The call-to-action is instruction on exactly what you want them to do. What is the action that you want them to take immediately after reading your LinkedIn message? A rule to follow: your call-to-action must be singular. Do not include multiple calls-to-action. That is far too aggressive for an initial cold LinkedIn message and can become overwhelming to the point that they simply do not respond at all. Do not drown your prospect in calls to action. You either want them to join with a free trial of your software or you want them to book an appointment. Figure out what the goal is and keep it singular. The call-to-action is the outcome of your cold LinkedIn message.

To recap, with just six steps, the anatomy of an effective cold LinkedIn message is very simple.

RCVSIC:

Research: Research the contact and company before you send a LinkedIn message.

Compliment: Drop a compliment about the contact or company in the first sentence of your LinkedIn message. Everyone's got something special.

Value proposition: Deliver a compelling, life-changing value proposition statement. "We help X do Y without W or Z." X equals persona, Y equals the biggest desired result, W equals pain one, Z equals pain two.

Social proof and credibility: Your logos, your case studies, your success stories, and your testimonials that you provide after the value proposition that helps people trust you.

Introduction: It's Aat B."Hi, It's Brandon at Seamless." "It's Jake at Marketo." "It's Sarah at Amazon." "It's Bethany at Google."

Call-to-action: Pencil in a call, scheduling a meeting, get them onto your software, secure an introduction, etc. Make the call to action singular. Then hit send.

Do not add anything else. This is the anatomy of a cold LinkedIn message. Cut out the fluff. Read it out loud, record yourself reading it out loud and delete anything that bloats the message.

When someone receives a LinkedIn message that's 17 paragraphs long, they feel waterboarded. It's too aggressive in the initial stages. There's no report, no relationship, no context, and no reason to spend the time.

Remember that they will be reading it on their mobile phone. It is too difficult to read paragraph, upon paragraph, upon paragraph on a mobile device. Space out every single sentence. Then after you've done RCVSIC and removed the fluff, then and only then can you hit send.

That is the anatomy of a perfect cold LinkedIn message. Lastly, you have to follow up. You can send the most amazing cold message of all time and still not receive an immediate response. People get busy. They don't have time in that exact moment to respond, and they forget. I get 100 LinkedIn messages a day, and so do your prospects.

Your prospects are slammed. When you send this perfect, six-step cold LinkedIn message, if you don't hear back, don't take it personally. Follow up, follow up, follow up.

In your follow up, leverage the anatomy of this cold LinkedIn message again. Go through your follow up. RCVSIC - Research, compliment, value prop, social proof and credibility, introduction, call-to-action.

Leverage this same framework every single time that you follow up, and I guarantee you, you will lock in that appointment, or lock in that call to action that you're looking for.

It may not happen on touch one, it may not happen on touch two, and even if it doesn't happen, that prospect knows that you care about their business, that you want to take them from where they're at today to where they want to go tomorrow, and even if they're not on the market at that time, guess what? They received 1,000 LinkedIn message, emails, cold calls, videos, texts that week, and you were the 1%, the one out of 1,000 that mastered the perfect persona-driven, research, value-driven social credibility, super-aligned pitch to take them from where they are today to where they need to go tomorrow, and they will remember that forever.

Even if you don't get a response, the impression alone, the impact, and the legacy that you build with each prospect because you took the time to follow this approach, will help them remember you. Anything hard is worth doing. Anyone can do the lazy thing. Anyone can send 10,000 cold emails to people without any research. Anyone can spray and pray 50,000 people.

Do you know what's really hard? Executing the anatomy of a perfect cold LinkedIn message by leveraging RCVSIC. That's hard. When you take the hard route, when you stop taking the easy road to success, you actually get there faster and you win bigger.

No massive accomplishment in this life was ever easy. Every entrepreneur, every salesperson, every marketer and recruiter that is part of the top 1%, they worked their asses off. I've studied them all. They have worked their asses off. Everyone in the top 1% works hard. They take the long road, they take the hard road. They don't take the easy road to success, because the easy road doesn't lead to success, it leads you down the mountain. The hard road leads you up the mountain, but you have to climb. You've got to climb Mount Everest. You got to get to the top, the top 1% of Mount Everest, which is you.

The anatomy of a hot, perfect LinkedIn message, RCVSIC, will get you there. It will help make that happen.

I want you to maximize your success, your potential, your revenue, your income, your sales, and the relationships that you build. I want to empower you to connect with opportunity. I want to positively impact a billion people, and I hope that this six-step framework for the anatomy of a perfect, cold LinkedIn message changes your life for the better.

Message Opening Lines

Listed below are a variety of great ways to open up and start a conversation on LinkedIn. It all starts with the opener on LinkedIn, so read, study, and get to work using these tested and proven opening lines today!

Great to virtually meet you …

Huge fan of …

Impressed with …

I appreciate all of the …

Big fan of your …

I noticed you …

{{*mutual connection*}} mentioned …

I saw that we both…

I loved your post on…

Congratulations on…

Impressed with your…

Amazing news on your…

I just saw in the news that…

Great post on …

{{*mutual connection*}} recommended we connect on …

Love what you guys are doing over there at {{*company*}} on …

Thanks for your post on {{*topic*}} yesterday …

{{*first_name*}} - love what you guys are doing at {{*company*}}

I wanted to share a new strategy to help you {{*value proposition*}}

Quick question about {{*first_name*}}...

{{*mutual connection*}} recommended we...

Congrats on the latest news about...

Ideas for {{*something that's important to them*}}

Question about {{*event*}}...

Question about {{*company goal*}}... Thoughts on {{*company growth strategy*}}

I wanted to share a quick strategy to help you accomplish {{*company goal*}}...

Thoughts about {{*title of their blog post*}}

Have you considered {{*thought/recommendation*}}? (not your service!)

{{*first_name*}} - quick question for you.

{{*referrer*}} said you might be able to answer this quick question.

Quick Question about {{*company*}}...

Thank you for signing up to test drive {{*sender company*}}...

Thanks for checking out {{*sender company*}}...

I recently read your blog post on {{*post title*}}...

Huge fan of your innovative {{*product*}} solutions...

Great job on...

Amazing work over there...

I want to help you {{*sender company value proposition*}}...

Loved the post on...

Congrats on the latest...

Big fan of your...

I'm really impressed with your...

Truly appreciate...

I recently came across {{*blog post title*}} that {{*you/your company. wrote/shared/posted*}} on {{*social media platform*}}...

{{*topic of blog post*}} seems like a great common interest/passion that we share. In fact, {{*one sentence comment on/reaction to blog post*}}.

SOCIAL SELLING SCRIPTS

Listed below are examples of complete messages you can send directly to a prospect or person of interest on LinkedIn. They are ready to copy, paste, and customize so you can learn to make millions with *Seven Figure Social Selling*!

DIRECT MESSAGE SCRIPTS

Direct Message 1:

Hey! I am a huge fan of your work {{*first_name*}}. You have definitely inspired me to _____ . I'd love to ask you more about _____ . When can we connect?

Direct Message 2:

Hi {{*first_name*}} - {{*Mutual connection*}} mentioned you were looking to grow your customer base. He felt I had a great solution that would allow you to do that and sent me your way. Do you have time for a phone call later today? I'd love to see how I can help you meet your goals.

Direct Message 3:

Hey {{*first_name*}} - I saw that we both attended {{*event*}}. I'd love to hear what you thought about it as a leader in {{*industry*}}. What were your main reasons for attending the event?

Direct Message 4:

Hey {{*first_name*}} - I'm impressed with your recent growth and traction online. Your story alone would go VIRAL on social media. I actually just helped {{*customer*}} go from _____ to_____ using {{*tool*}}. What would it take to let me help you reach more {{*customers*}} than ever before? Let me know if there is a better way to reach you than LinkedIn messages. Let's make it happen!!

Direct Message 5:

Amazing news on {{*company launch/company reunion/ company's IPO*}}. It is my dream to be a part of your company's expansion. I excel at _____ .

Who at your company is the best person to talk to about this?

Direct Message 6:

Great post on {{*topic*}}! I really enjoyed the insight you provided. I'd love to {{*goal*}}. My favorite part was: {{*details*}}. Going to call you asap, because there's something CRAZY I need to connect with you regarding this. Best phone number?

Direct Message 7:

Hey {{*first_name*}} - I noticed you reached {{*goal*}} - WOW! I just helped {{*mutual connection*}} cross over from {{*number*}} to {{*number*}} in {{*timeframe*}}. Record-breaking!! Just wanted to let you know if you're ever interested in tripling your {{*objective*}}, you know where to find me!

Hope you have a great day!

Direct Message 8:

Thanks for your post on {{*topic*}} yesterday, it really impacted me in a positive way. Would you be willing to {{*goal*}}? I'd love to see if there is a possibility of working together in the future.

Direct Message 9:

{{*first_name*}} - This may not be a priority for you, but I just broke ground with a new strategy helping companies just like yours {{*value. proposition*}}. I know you're busy, but I would hate you to miss out. What do you think? Any interest?

Direct Message 10:

Hi {{*first_name*}} - LOVE what your company is up to lately!! As someone who is obsessed with {{*industry*}}, I couldn't help but dig deeper… (WOA!) You have no idea how much gold I just found…

My findings:

Compliment, problem, solution
Compliment, problem, solution
Compliment problem, solution

So fascinated by you guys… what are your goals this year? Keep doing what you're doing!!!

CONNECTION REQUESTS SCRIPTS, COLD

Connection Request Cold 1:

Hi {{*first_name*}} - I love connecting with inspiring {{*recipient role*}} and experts out to make a difference in the world!

I stumbled on your profile, and it seems we have many things in common like {{*traits, experience, etc*}}.

I look forward to becoming a valuable connection for you and your work too!

All the Best,

{{*your_name*}}

Connection Request
Cold 2:

{{*first_name*}} - It was great meeting you and I look forward to the opportunity to work together. In the meantime, I'd like to add you to my network on LinkedIn.

If any of my connections can ever help you out in any way, please let me know and I'll be more than happy to make introductions.

Best,

{{*your_name*}}

Connection Request
Cold 3:

{{*first_name*}} - Great to virtually meet you! I noticed we socialize in similar circles with our experience and think it'd be beneficial to connect here on LinkedIn!

If any of my connections can ever help you out in any way, please let me know so I can make an introduction and help streamline your success!

Best, {{*your_name*}}

Connection Request Cold 4:

{{*first_name*}} - I'm really impressed with your innovative {{*company product*}} solutions at {{*company*}} and would love to connect here on LinkedIn.

If anyone in my network can be of value to you, let me know and I'd be happy to make that happen.

All the Best,

{{*your_name*}}

Connection Request
Cold 5:

Hi {{*first_name*}} - I'm excited to connect. {{*personal compliment*}}. I can really relate with your {{*most recent post link*}}.

Great minds think alike {{*link to your post*}}.

I would love to keep in touch and will continue to enjoy your content.

Talk soon!

{{*your_name*}}

Connection Request
Cold 6:

Hi {{*first_name*}} - Happy {{*today*}}! Didn't want to let another day go by without requesting a connection.

I heard about what you do with {{*event/person/company*}} and was super excited about how much we have in common.

Would love to connect here and see how we might be able to align on {{*projects/connections*}}.

Let me know how I can help. Thanks for being a new part of my network!

Cheers,

{{*your_name*}}

Connection Request
Cold 7:

Hi {{*first_name*}} - I'm impressed with your background as {{*title*}} at companies like {{*contact current company*}}, {{*contact past company*}} and others.

I'd like to add you to my network here on LinkedIn and learn as much as possible from all your valuable posts.

In the meantime, if any of my connections can ever help you out in any way, please let me know and I'll be more than happy to make introductions.

Sending my Best,

{{*your_name*}}

Connection Request
Cold 8:

Hey {{*first_name*}} - I was recently connecting with {{*common connection*}} and they suggested I check out your profile. I'm glad I did.

It looks like we socialize in similar circles and have over {{*number of connections*}} shared connections.

It would be great to connect with you and network here on LI.

If anyone in my circle can ever help you out, just let me know, and I'll be happy to make an intro.

Best,

{{*your_name*}}

Connection Request Cold 9:

{{*first_name*}} - There is a fine line between good prospecting and bad manners, and I don't want to cross over to the latter.

I've tried several times to connect with you. Unfortunately, I haven't had any luck and I don't want to come off as a pest.

I would feel bad if I kept messaging you so I am going to back off for now unless you tell me otherwise.

I'll leave you with this.

{{*insert a bold pitch statement*}}.

We are the {{*insert how you are set apart in the industry*}} and {{*value proposition*}}.

Imagine if your {{*department*}} could increase {{*objective*}} by {{*percent*}}. Last chance, can we discuss {{*your product or solution*}}?

Layer:

If not, please just reply here and let me know. We can keep in touch and if your needs change or we can ever be of assistance, please keep us at the top of your list and don't hesitate to reach out anytime.

Thank you for your time.

{{*your_name*}}

Connection Request Cold 10:

Hi {{*first_name*}} - I'll be straight up with you.

{{*sender unique selling proposition*}}. I want to help you crush your {{*objective*}} and capture your {{*goal*}} this year.

Our platform will help you {{*unique benefit*}}.

Let me know what I can do to ensure you succeed today,

{{*your_name*}}

COLD PITCH SCRIPTS

Cold Pitch 1:

Hi {{*first_name*}} - I wanted to congratulate you on the latest {{*company news*}}! What an

accomplishment! Definitely something to celebrate and be proud of.

I couldn't help but wonder if you are looking to scale and to increase {{*sender product results*}}?

I help companies {{*sender company results*}} without {{*pain*}} in {{*time*}} months or less.

We've helped {{*industry*}} companies like {{*sender company client 1, 2, 3*}} and many others maximize their results. I know we can do the same for you.

At this stage in your success with {{*company*}}, I'd love to hear what you think. It would be great to share more over a quick 5 min call next week.

Cheers,

{{*your_name*}}

Cold Pitch 2:

Hi {{*first_name*}} - Happy {{*today*}} and congrats on all your recent success in {{*company news*}}!

I'm curious about what your current goals and projects are right now. It looks like you are in a great position to really level up.

Are you looking for strategies to increase {{*sender product results*}}?

I help companies {{*sender company results*}} without {{*pain 1,2,3*}} in {{*time*}} months or less.

We've helped {{*industry*}} companies like {{*sender company client 1, 2, 3*}} and many others maximize their results. I am absolutely certain we can do the same for you, or I wouldn't be reaching out.

Let me know if you have any interest. It would be great to share more over a quick 5 min call next week.

Thanks and hope to chat more soon!
{{your_name}}

Cold Pitch 3:

Hi *{{first_name}}* - Big fan of *{{company}}* and all you are doing to solve *{{problem}}*. You are really making a difference in *{{industry}}* and I have loved following your work.

I was researching how *{{company}}* helps customers *{{company results}}* and thought you might be interested in *{{sender company value proposition}}*.

Are you looking for strategies to increase *{{sender product results}}*? I help companies *{{sender company results}}* without *{{pain 1, 2, or 3}}*.

We've helped *{{industry}}* companies like *{{sender company client 1, 2, 3}}* and others increase results by *{{sender product results}}*. I want to do the same for you.

Please let me know when you'd like to talk. It'd be great to share more over a quick 5 min call next week.

Sending my Best,
{{*your_name*}}

Cold Pitch 4:

Hi {{*first_name*}} - Thank you for connecting! I see you guys have been up to some really innovative things over at {{*company*}}!

I'm sure there are exciting times ahead! What are your next big moves this year?

I wanted to reach out primarily because we've been seeing a lot of companies like you guys increase {{*your product results*}} using {{*your solution*}}.

I help companies {{*sender company results*}} without {{*pain 1, 2*}} in {{*time*}} months or less.

We've helped {{*industry*}} companies like {{*sender company client 1, 2, 3*}} and many others maximize their results and I know we can do the same for you!

(If local) - Are you in the area this week?

Let me know what you think! It'd be great to share more over a quick 5 min call next week or {{*meeting place suggestion*}}.

Grateful to connect with you and look forward to the possibilities,
{{*your_name*}}

Cold Pitch 5:

Hi {{*first_name*}} - Thank you for connecting! I just took a look at your website and am really impressed.

In fact, a lot of your content aligns perfectly with {{*sender company goals*}}. I see you guys have been up to some really innovative things over at {{*company*}}!

What are your goals this year? I wanted to reach out mainly because we've been seeing a lot of companies like yours increase {{*product results*}} using {{*your solution*}}.

I help companies {{*sender company results*}} without {{*pain 1, 2, 3*}} in {{*time*}} or less.

We've helped {{*industry*}} companies like {{*sender company client 1, 2, 3*}} and many others maximize their results and I would love to do the same for you.

Let me know what you think! It'd be great to share more over a quick 5 min call next week.

Looking forward to it!

{{*your_name*}}

Cold Pitch 6:

Hi {{*first_name*}} - I loved reading your latest post about {{*topic*}} and really want to connect. I think it would be great to discuss options of working together to {{*goal*}} and see if there is any way I can support you in {{*growth idea*}}.

Do you know what your company's current goals are for {{*growth goal*}}?

I've helped several companies like yours achieve {{*company results*}} and after looking over what you do at {{*account name*}}, I know I could help you do the same.

I've worked with {{*industry*}} companies like {{*company 1, 2, 3*}} and have helped them resolve {{*pain 1, 2*}} in as little as {{*time*}} or less.

Let me know if this is something you are interested in pursuing and we can set up a time for me to call you personally.

I look forward to hearing from you!

{{*your_name*}}

Cold Pitch 7:

Hi {{*first_name*}} - {{*shared connection*}} told me a lot about what you do and I had to reach out. They had so many great things to say about you. I think we have a lot in common and I would love to see if there is any potential in working together in the near future.

Do you have current goals for {{*growth goal*}}? I think if we teamed up we could really make a difference for you and {{*company*}}.

I've been working with companies for {{*time*}} years helping them {{*company results*}} and would love to do the same for you.

Companies I've worked with include {{*company 1, 2, 3*}} and we have successfully resolved {{*pain 1, 2*}}. The best part is, it only took about {{*time*}} months.

Let me know if this is something you feel drawn to and we can set up a time for me to call you personally.

I look forward to hearing from you!

{{*your_name*}}

Cold Pitch 8:

Hi {{*first_name*}} - I saw that you're working for {{*recipient's company*}} and I had to reach out. I have worked with companies like yours in the past and I would love to see if there is any potential for us to work together in the near future.

Can you tell me what your current goals are for the year?

I know how to take companies out of {{*pain 1, 2, 3*}} in as little as {{*time*}}.

Companies I've worked with include {{*company 1, 2, 3*}} which seem to have had similar challenges as {{*account name*}}.

Let me know if this is something you feel you'd like to see more of and we can set up a time for me to call you personally.

I look forward to hearing from you!

{{*your_name*}}

Cold Pitch 9:

Hi {{*first_name*}} - I am so intrigued by your extensive work experience in {{*account industry*}}. I would love to connect and see what I can do to help you reach your goals this year.

I've been working with companies for {{*time*}} helping them {{*company results*}} and would love to do the same for you.

These companies include but are not limited to, {{*company 1, 2, 3*}} and we have successfully resolved {{*pain 1, 2*}}. We did all this in only {{*time*}}, and I would not be reaching out if I didn't know for sure that I can help you do the same. I want to show you how to go from _____ to _____ .

Let me know if this is something you would be interested in because I'd really like to set up a time for me to call you personally.

I look forward to hearing from you!

Sending my Best,
{{*your_name*}}

Cold Pitch 10:

Hi {{*first_name*}} - I noticed you have followers on LI - CRAZY! I put together a list of top industry experts to give {{*product/service*}} away for just {{*special promo*}} in exchange for some feedback. I came across your profile and know you'll be perfect for this. Our company {{*pitch or mission statement*}}

Here's how we can help - {{*sender company case studies*}}

I'd love to put my money where my mouth is and give your team {{*special promotion*}}.

No credit card, no demo, no catch.

(Instruct how to sign up)

*Example:

Take advantage of {{*special promotion*}}

using referral code: {{*promo code*}}

Please let me know if you have any questions.

{{*your_name*}}

CONNECTION REQUEST SCRIPTS, VISITED YOUR PROFILE

Connection Request Visited Your Profile 1:

Thanks so much for visiting my profile! I'd like to add you to my network here on LinkedIn.

If any of my connections can ever help you out in any way, please let me know & I'd be more than happy to make introductions.

{{your_name}}

Connection Request
Visited Your Profile 2:

Thanks for visiting my profile! It looks like we have a lot of common interests & shared connections. I'd like to add you to my network here on LinkedIn.

If any of my connections can ever help you out in any way, please let me know & I'd be more than happy to make introductions.

Best,
{{*your_name*}}

Connection Request
Visited Your Profile 3:

Hi {{*first_name*}} - Happy {{*today*}}. It's great to connect! I noticed you visited my profile. I always like to connect and help like-minded people in my network.

If any of my connections can ever help you out in any way, please let me know & I'd be more than happy to make introductions.

My Best,

{{*your_name*}}

Connection Request Visited Your Profile 4:

Hi {{*first_name*}} - I hope this finds you well.

I just noticed you stopped by my profile. Is there anything that I can specifically help you with?

In the meantime, it would be great to connect here on LinkedIn. If any of my connections can ever help you out in any way, please let me know & I'd be more than happy to make introductions.

Best,

{{*your_name*}}

Connection Request
Visited Your Profile 5:

Hi {{*first_name*}} - I noticed that you stopped by my profile and I'm so glad you did. If there is anything I can help you with specifically, please let me know.

Otherwise, it's still great to be connected here on LinkedIn. If any of my connections can ever help you out in any way, please let me know & I'd be more than happy to make introductions.

Best,
{{*your_name*}}

Connection Request
Visited Your Profile 6:

Hi {{*first_name*}} - I'm so glad you stopped by my profile. It looks like we have quite a few shared connections and interests.

I'd love to stay connected here on LinkedIn. If any of my connections can ever help you out in any way, please let me know & I'd be more than happy to make introductions.

Best,

{{*your_name*}}

Connection Request Visited Your Profile 7:

Hi {{*first_name*}} - I'm glad you stopped by my profile today. It looks like we have a lot in common.

Let's stay connected here on LinkedIn. I'm excited to watch you progress professionally. If any of my connections can ever help you out in any way, please let me know & I'd be more than happy to make introductions.

Best,

{{*your_name*}}

Connection Request
Visited Your Profile 8:

Hi {{*first_name*}} - Thanks for checking out my profile! I took a look at yours too and it seems like we share a lot of the same work experience.

Let's keep in touch here on LinkedIn. I'm excited to watch you progress professionally. If any of my connections can ever help you out in any way, please let me know & I'd be more than happy to make introductions.

Best,
{{*your_name*}}

Connection Request
Visited Your Profile 9:

Hi {{*first_name*}} - Thanks for visiting my profile. I just looked through yours as well and wow! I'm very impressed!

Let's definitely stay connected here on LinkedIn. If any of my connections can ever help you out in any way, please let me know & I'd be more than happy to make introductions.

Best,

{{*your_name*}}

Connection Request Visited Your Profile 10:

Hi {{*first_name*}} - Thank you so much for stopping by my page today. I love connecting with like- minded people on this platform.

I'd really like to connect here with you on LinkedIn. If any of my connections can ever help you out in any way, please let me know & I'd be more than happy to make introductions.

Best,

{{*your_name*}}

CONNECTION REQUEST SCRIPTS, LIKED YOUR PROFILE

Connection Request Liked Your Profile 1:

Thanks so much for following my content and liking my profile! I'd like to add you to my network here on LinkedIn.

If any of my connections can ever help you out in any way, please let me know & I'd be more than happy to make introductions.

Best,

{{your_name}}

Connection Request Liked Your Profile 2:

Thanks so much for liking my profile! It only makes sense to add you here on LinkedIn.

If any of my connections can ever help you out in any way, please let me know & I'd be more than happy to make introductions.

Best,
{{*your_name*}}

Connection Request Liked Your Profile 3:

Thanks so much for liking my profile! It looks like we have many common interests & shared connections.

I'd like to add you to my network here on LinkedIn.

If any of my connections can ever help you out in any way, please let me know & I'd be more than happy to make introductions.

Best,

{{your_name}}

Connection Request
Liked Your Profile 4:

Great virtually meeting you and thanks for liking my profile on LinkedIn! I look forward to the opportunity to work together and would like to add you to my network on LinkedIn.

If any of my connections can ever help you out in any way, please let me know and I'll be more than happy to make introductions.

Best,

{{your_name}}

Connection Request Liked Your Profile 5:

Hi {{*first_name*}} - Thanks for following my content and liking my profile on LinkedIn. That truly means a lot to me, I appreciate you.

I'd like to add you to my network here on LinkedIn.

If any of my connections can ever help you out in any way, please let me know & I'd be more than happy to make introductions.

Best,

{{*your_name*}}

Connection Request Liked Your Profile 6:

Hi {{*first_name*}} - Thank you so much for supporting my content here on LinkedIn. I am excited to connect and do the same for you.

I'd love to add you to my network here on LinkedIn.

If any of my connections can ever help you out in any way, please let me know & I'd be more than happy to make introductions.

Best,

{{your_name}}

Connection Request Liked Your Profile 7:

{{first_name}} - Thank you so much for showing some love on my profile today. I'm glad it resonated with you.

I'd like to add you to my network here on LinkedIn.

If any of my connections can ever help you out in any way, please let me know & I'd be more than happy to make introductions.

Best,

{{your_name}}

Connection Request
Liked Your Profile 8:

{{*first_name*}} - Thank you so much for engaging on my latest profile. It looks like we have a lot in common.

I'd like to add you to my network here on LinkedIn.

If any of my connections can ever help you out in any way, please let me know & I'd be more than happy to make introductions.

Best,
{{*your_name*}}

Connection Request
Liked Your Profile 9:

{{*first_name*}} - I'm so glad you like my profile! I took a look at your profile and we seem to be interested in a lot of the same things.

I'd like to add you to my network here on LinkedIn.

If you ever find you need an introduction from me, I'm happy to share my network with you.

Best,

{{*your_name*}}

Connection Request
Liked Your Profile 10:

{{*first_name*}} - Thank you for taking the time to engage with my profile here on LinkedIn. It means a lot to me.

I'd like to add you to my network here on LinkedIn.

If any of my connections can ever help you out in any way, please let me know & I'd be more than happy to make introductions.

Best,

{{*your_name*}}

INVITE REQUEST SCRIPTS, LIKED POST

Invite Request Liked Post 1:

Hey {{*first_name*}} - Great virtually meeting you and thank you for liking my post! I'd like to add you to my network on LinkedIn.

If any of my connections can ever help you out in any way, please let me know and I'll be more than happy to make introductions.

Best,

{{*your_name*}}

Invite Request
Liked Post 2:

Hey {{*first_name*}} - Thank you for liking my post! It means a lot when people take the time to engage with my content. I'd love to add you to my network on LinkedIn.

If any of my connections can ever help you out in any way, please let me know and I'll be more than happy to make introductions.

Best,
{{*your_name*}}

Invite Request
Liked Post 3:

Hey {{*first_name*}} - Thank you so much for liking my post! It looks like we share quite a bit in common. Let's add each other here on LinkedIn.

If any of my connections can ever help you out in any way, please let me know and I'll be more than happy to make introductions.

Best, {{*your_name*}}

Invite Request Liked Post 4:

Hey {{*first_name*}} - I noticed you liked my post earlier today. Thank you! Tell me, what was your favorite takeaway? I'd love to add you to my network on LinkedIn.

If any of my connections can ever help you out in any way, please let me know and I'll be more than happy to make introductions.

Best,

{{*your_name*}}

Invite Request
Liked Post 5:

Hi {{*first_name*}} - I really appreciate you taking the time to like my post and I'd love to add you to my network on LinkedIn.

If any of my connections can ever help you out in any way, please let me know and I'll be more than happy to make introductions.

Best,
{{*your_name*}}

Invite Request
Liked Post 6:

Hey {{*first_name*}} - Thank you for liking my post! I am so glad it resonated with you. I'd love to add you to my network on LinkedIn.

If any of my connections can ever help you out in any way, please let me know and I'll be more than happy to make introductions.

Best,

{{*your_name*}}

Invite Request
Liked Post 7:

Hey {{*first_name*}} - So grateful that you took the time to like my post! It means a lot when my

content resonates with others. I'd love to add you to my network on LinkedIn and see if there is any way I can further support you.

If any of my connections can ever help you out in any way, please let me know and I'll be more than happy to make introductions.

Best,

{{*your_name*}}

Invite Request
Liked Post 8:

Hey {{*first_name*}} - Thank you for liking my post!

I'd love to stay connected here on LinkedIn. It's fun to find other {{*industry*}} professionals with similar interests and experience.

If any of my connections can ever help you out in any way, please let me know and I'll be more than happy to make introductions.

Best,

{{*your_name*}}

Invite Request
Liked Post 9:

Hey {{*first_name*}} - Thanks for pausing to like my post today! Let's connect!

Let me know if I can ever make introductions to others you think could help you out.

Best,

{{*your_name*}}

Invite Request
Liked Post 10:

Hey {{*first_name*}} - Thank you for liking my post! I'd love to add you to my network on LinkedIn and stay in touch. It looks like we share similar interests surrounding {{*topic*}}.

If any of my connections can ever help you out in any way, please let me know and I'll be more than happy to make introductions.

Best,

{{*your_name*}}

CONNECTION REQUEST SCRIPTS, SHARED YOUR ARTICLE

Connection Request Shared Your Article 1:

Thank you so much for sharing my article! I'd like to add you to my network here on LinkedIn.

Do you see any connections in my network that could be of value for you? Let me know if I can help make that happen.

Best,

{{your_name}}

Connection Request
Shared Your Article 2:

Thank you for sharing my article! I'd like to add you to my network here on LinkedIn.

If any of my connections can ever help you out in any way, please let me know & I'd be more than happy to make introductions.

Best,

{{*your_name*}}

Connection Request
Shared Your Article 3:

Wow! Thank you for sharing my article today! It looks like we have many common interests & shared connections.

I'd like to add you to my network here on LinkedIn.

Any connection of mine is a connection of yours, so as always, let me know how I can help you out.

Best,

{{your_name}}

Connection Request Shared Your Article 4:

Great virtually meeting you and thanks for sharing my article on LinkedIn! I look forward to the opportunity to work together and would like to add you to my network on LinkedIn.

If any of my connections can ever help you out in any way, please let me know and I'll be more than happy to make introductions.

Best,

{{your_name}}

Connection Request
Shared Your Article 5:

Hi {{*first_name*}} - Thanks for following my content and liking my post on LinkedIn. That truly means a lot to me and I appreciate you.

I'd like to add you to my network here on LinkedIn.

If any of my connections can ever help you out in any way, please let me know & I'd be more than happy to make introductions.

Best,

{{*your_name*}}

Connection Request
Shared Your Article 6:

Hi {{*first_name*}} - Thank you so much for supporting my content and sharing my article here on LinkedIn. I am excited to connect and do the same for you.

I'd love to add you to my network here on LinkedIn.

As an ice-breaker, what are some of your company goals this year?

Best,

{{*your_name*}}

Connection Request
Shared Your Article 7:

{{*first_name*}} - Thank you so much for showing some love and sharing my post today. I'm glad it resonated with you.

I'd like to add you to my network here on LinkedIn.

If any of my connections can support you in {{*goals*}} this year, please let me know & I'd be more than happy to make introductions.

Best,

{{*your_name*}}

Connection Request
Shared Your Article 8:

{{*first_name*}} - Thank you so much for engaging with and sharing my latest article. It looks like we have a lot in common.

I'd like to add you to my network here on LinkedIn.

While we're at it, take a quick look at my connections and let me know if you ever need me to make a quick introduction.

Best,

{{*your_name*}}

Connection Request
Shared Your Article 9:

{{*first_name*}} - I'm so glad you liked my latest post! Thank you for sharing it! I took a look at your profile and we seem to be interested in a lot of the same things.

I'd like to add you to my network here on LinkedIn.

Let's stay in touch and share connections when it makes sense to help one another out.

Best,

{{*your_name*}}

Connection Request
Shared Your Article 10:

{{*first_name*}} - Thank you for taking the time to engage with and share my content here on LinkedIn. What struck you the most?

I'd like to add you to my network on LinkedIn.

If any of my connections can ever help you out in any way, please let me know & I'd be more than happy to make introductions.

Best,

{{*your_name*}}

CONNECTION REQUEST SCRIPTS, MUTUAL CONNECT

Connection Request Mutual Connect 1:

{{*first_name*}} - {{*Mutual connection*}} recommended we connect as we both do a lot of work in the {{*industry*}} space.

It'd be great to add each other here on LinkedIn.

If anyone in my network can ever help you out in any way, let me know and I'd be happy to make introductions.

Best,

{{*your_name*}}

Connection Request Mutual Connect 2:

Hi {{*first_name*}} - Great to virtually connect here on LI.

I was at the {{*event*}} where I was speaking with {{*mutual connection*}} and they recommended we connect as we both do a lot of work in the {{*industry*}} space.

It'd be great to connect here on LinkedIn.

If anyone in my network can ever help you out in any way, let me know and I'd be happy to make introductions.

Best,

{{*your_name*}}

Connection Request Mutual Connect 3:

{{*first_name*}} - {{*Mutual connection*}} suggested I reach out to you as we both do a lot of work in the {{*industry*}} space.

It'd be great to add each other here on LinkedIn.

If anyone in my network can ever help you out in any way, let me know and I'd be happy to make introductions.

Best,

{{*your_name*}}

Connection Request Mutual Connect 4:

{{*first_name*}} - Our friend {{*mutual connection*}} recommended we connect. He/she told me what you are doing in {{*industry*}} and I am super impressed.

It'd be great to add each other here on LinkedIn.

If you see anyone in my network you have been wanting to connect with, I would have happy to make that introduction happen.

Best,

{{*your_name*}}

Connection Request Mutual Connect 5:

{{*first_name*}} - {{*Mutual connection*}} recommended we connect. They told me what you are doing in {{*industry*}} and I would love to see if there is anything I can do to further {{*goal*}}.

It would be great to add each other here on LinkedIn.

Let me know the best way to keep in touch and/or if you'd like to get a quick call on the books.

Otherwise, I look forward to sharing connections and helping one another grow.

Best,

{{*your_name*}}

Connection Request
Mutual Connect 6:

{{*first_name*}} - {{*Mutual connection*}} told me what you are doing in {{*industry*}} and I wanted to reach out to see if there is anything I can do to help support you. Looks like we share a lot of similar experiences.

I'd love to add each other here on LinkedIn.

If anyone in my network can ever help you out in any way, let me know and I'd be happy to make introductions.

Best,

{{*your_name*}}

Connection Request
Mutual Connect 7:

{{*first_name*}} - Our friend {{*mutual connection*}} mentioned {{*shared experience*}}. I also {{*shared experience*}}!

I'd love to connect here on LinkedIn.

If anyone in my network can ever help you out in any way, let me know and I'd be happy to make introductions.

Best,

{{*your_name*}}

Connection Request Mutual Connect 8:

{{*first_name*}} - I'm reaching out today because {{*mutual connection*}} recommended we connect. They told me what you are doing in {{*industry*}} and I am super impressed.

It would be great to add each other here on LinkedIn!

Best,

{{*your_name*}}

Connection Request
Mutual Connect 9:

{{*first_name*}} - {{*Mutual connection*}} insisted I reach out to you. They told me you are also working in {{*industry*}} and that you are absolutely crushing it. I'd love to learn from you.

Let's add each other here on LinkedIn.

If anyone in my network can ever help you out in any way, let me know and I'd be happy to make introductions.

Best,

{{*your_name*}}

Connection Request
Mutual Connect 10:

{{*first_name*}} - {{*Mutual connection*}} has told me so much about you. I'd love to meet sometime and talk to you more about what you are doing in {{*industry*}} space.

Let's add each other here on LinkedIn. I'm free

{{*days/times*}}. How about you?

Best,

{{*your_name*}}

CONNECTION REQUEST SCRIPTS, COWORKERS

Connection Request Coworkers 1:

I noticed we both work here at {{*company*}}! I'd love to follow your great posts and connect with you here on LinkedIn.

If any of my connections can ever help you out in any way, please let me know & I'd be more than happy to make introductions.

Best,

{{*your_name*}}

Connection Request Coworkers 2:

I noticed we both work here at {{*company*}}! It'd be great to connect here on LinkedIn!

Thank you for all your hard work, and I look forward to working with you.

Best,

{{*your_name*}}

Connection Request Coworkers 3:

Hi {{*first_name*}} - Great to meet you! I noticed we both work here at {{*company*}} so it would be great to connect here on LinkedIn.

If I or any of my connections can ever help you out in any way, please let me know & I'd be more than happy to make introductions.

Best,

{{*your_name*}}

Connection Request
Coworkers 4:

Hi {{*first_name*}} - I'm networking with other coworkers from {{*company*}} here on LI and noticed we haven't connected yet!

Looking forward to your updates and helping you succeed in whatever ways I can assist.

Best,

{{*your_name*}}

Connection Request
Coworkers 5:

Hi {{*first_name*}} - I'm connecting with other coworkers from {{*company*}} here on LI and noticed we haven't virtually met yet!

I'd love to know more about you.

Let me know how I can help out, and as always, my connections are your connections. I am always happy to make any introductions you may be looking for.

Best,

{{*your_name*}}

Connection Request Coworkers 6:

Hi {{*first_name*}} - I'm networking with other coworkers from {{*company*}} here on LI and noticed we haven't connected yet!

It'd be great to connect and follow all you're doing professionally for {{*company*}}. If there is anything

I can ever do to help further your goals, please let me know.

Best,

{{*your_name*}}

Connection Request
Coworkers 7:

Hi {{*first_name*}} - I'm reaching out to other coworkers from {{*company*}} here on LI and wanted to make sure we connected.

If I or any of my connections can ever help you out in any way, please let me know & I'd be more than happy to make introductions or do whatever I can to support you.

Best,

{{*your_name*}}

Connection Request
Coworkers 8:

Hi {{*first_name*}} - I'd like to get to know other coworkers from {{*company*}} here on LI and thought I'd reach out.

It would be great to connect. If I or any of my connections can ever help you out in any way, please let me know & I'd be more than happy to make introductions or help you reach your goals however I can.

Best,

{{*your_name*}}

Connection Request Coworkers 9:

Hi {{*first_name*}} - I noticed you also work for {{*company*}} and I wanted to connect here on LI.

I'd love to help and support you any way I can. Let me know how I can make that happen. I'm excited to follow and learn from you!

Best,

{{*your_name*}}

Connection Request
Coworkers 10:

Hi {{*first_name*}} - I want to get in touch with other coworkers from {{*company*}} here on LI. Your profile caught my eye and I wanted to make sure we connected.

If I or any of my connections can ever help you out in any way, please let me know & I'd be more than happy to make introductions or help out however I can.

Best,

{{*your_name*}}

CONNECTION REQUEST SCRIPTS, WRITER, AUTHOR, REPORTER, SPEAKER

Connection Request
Writer, Author, Reporter, Speaker 1:

{{*first_name*}} - I am such a big fan of your content and would love to connect here on LinkedIn to follow and learn more.

If any of my connections can ever help you out in any way, please let me know & I'd be more than happy to make introductions.

Best,

{{*your_name*}}

Connection Request
Writer, Author, Reporter, Speaker 2:

{{*first_name*}} - I am a huge fan of your content and would love to connect here on LinkedIn!

If you ever see someone in my network you'd like me to help introduce you to, I'm always happy to do that.

Best,

{{*your_name*}}

Connection Request
Writer, Author, Reporter, Speaker 3:

{{*first_name*}} - I just finished reading your great content on {{*topic*}} and wanted to say thanks so much for sharing!

It'd be an honor to connect with you here on LinkedIn. If any of my connections can ever support your work or help you out in any way, please let me know.

Best,

{{*your_name*}}

Connection Request
Writer, Author, Reporter, Speaker 4:

{{*first_name*}} - I'm a big fan of your content and wanted to say thanks so much for sharing!

It'd be an honor to connect with you here on LinkedIn & if any of my connections can ever help you out in any way, please let me know.

Best,

{{*your_name*}}

Connection Request
Writer, Author, Reporter, Speaker 5:

Hi {{*first_name*}} - I really enjoyed your posts on {{*topic*}}! I've got a list of great takeaways from it that I'm going to apply right away.

Anyways, It would be great to connect here and follow more of your content.

If any of my connections can ever help you out in any way, please let me know.

Best,

{{your_name}}

Connection Request
Writer, Author, Reporter, Speaker 6:

Hi *{{first_name}}* - Great post today on *{{topic}}*! I'd love to continue following your content and connect here on LinkedIn.

If any of my connections can ever help you out in any way, please let me know & I'd be more than happy to make introductions.

Best,

{{your_name}}

Connection Request
Writer, Author, Reporter, Speaker 7:

Hi {{*first_name*}} - Great post today on {{*topic*}}! I learned a lot!

I look forward to connecting here on LinkedIn and following more of your great content!

If you ever see anyone worth connecting with in my circle, please don't hesitate to reach out!

Best,

{{*your_name*}}

Connection Request
Writer, Author, Reporter, Speaker 8:

Hi {{*first_name*}} - Really loved your post today on {{*topic*}}! I never thought about how {{*insight*}}. Thank you for sharing!

I look forward to connecting here on LinkedIn and following more of your great content!

If any of my connections can ever help you out in any way, please let me know & I'd be more than happy to make introductions.

Best,

{{*your_name*}}

Connection Request
Writer, Author, Reporter, Speaker 9:

Hi {{*first_name*}} - Awesome post on {{*topic*}}! I specifically loved the part about _____ .

I am so happy to be able to connect here on LinkedIn so I can follow and learn more from you.

Let me know if any connections I have could be helpful to you. Always happy to make introductions.

Best,

{{*your_name*}}

Connection Request
Writer, Author, Reporter, Speaker 10:

Hi {{*first_name*}} - Your post today on {{*topic*}} was so strong. It really grabbed my attention.

I'd love to connect here on LinkedIn and so I can follow more of your posts and gain new insight.

Also, I'm happy to share introductions if you're ever interested in connecting with others in my network.

Best,

{{*your_name*}}

CONNECTION REQUEST SCRIPTS, EDUCATION

Connection Request Education 1:

I noticed we both studied at {{*college*}}! I'd love to follow your great posts and connect with you here on LinkedIn.

If any of my connections can ever help you out in any way, please let me know & I'd be more than happy to make introductions.

Best,

{{*your_name*}}

Connection Request Education 2:

I noticed we both went to school at {{*college*}}! It'd be great to connect here on LinkedIn!

If any of my connections can ever help you out in any way, please let me know & I'd be more than happy to make introductions.

Best,

{{*your_name*}}

Connection Request Education 3:

Go {{*school mascot*}}!

Hi {{*first_name*}} - I recognized we socialize in similar circles and also went to the same alma mater.

It would be great to connect here on LinkedIn!

If anyone in my network can ever help you out, please let me know.

All the Best,

{{*your_name*}}

Connection Request
Education 4:

Hi {{*first_name*}} - I'm impressed with your background working at {{*current company*}} and {{*past company*}}.

Additionally, I noticed we both went to the same college.

It'd be great to connect here and if anyone in my network can help you, just let me know.

Best,

{{*your_name*}}

Connection Request
Education 5:

Go {{*school mascot*}}! I noticed we both went to school at {{*college*}} and have similar social circles and interests.

It'd be great to connect here on LinkedIn and network.

If any of my connections can ever help you out in any way, please let me know & I'd be more than happy to make introductions.

Best,

{{*your_name*}}

Connection Request Education 6:

Hi {{*first_name*}} - I noticed we both went to {{*college*}}. I hope your time there was as great as mine. I'll never forget {{*specific college tradition*}}.

It'd be great to connect here and if anyone in my network can help you, just let me know.

Best,

{{*your_name*}}

Connection Request
Education 7:

Hi {{*first_name*}} - I love connecting with people who also attended {{*college*}}.

I think it's great to be able to help each other out as we grow professionally.

It'd be great to connect here and if anyone in my network can help you, just let me know.

Best,
{{*your_name*}}

Connection Request
Education 8:

Hi {{*first_name*}} - Your profile caught my eye and I noticed we both went to {{*college*}}.

I'd love to keep in touch here on LinkedIn.

Please let me know if I or anyone in my network can help you. I'd be happy to make the introduction.

Best,

{{*your_name*}}

Connection Request Education 9:

Hi {{*first_name*}} - I'm super impressed with your work experience since attending {{*college*}}. I also graduated from {{*college*}}!

I noticed we have a lot in common.

I'd love to connect here on LI. If anyone in my network can help you, just let me know!

Best,

{{*your_name*}}

Connection Request Education 10:

Hi {{*first_name*}} - Love finding other {{*industry*}} professionals who also graduated from {{*college*}}!

Let's connect here on LinkedIn and help each other grow professionally. If anyone in my network can help you, please let me know. I'd love to make the introduction.

Best,

{{*your_name*}}

CONNECTION REQUEST MESSAGE SCRIPTS, FRATERNITY/SORORITY

Connection Request Message Fraternity/Sorority 1:

Hi {{*first_name*}} - I noticed you are also a part of {{*fraternity/sorority*}}! I love connecting with fellow alumni! Let's add each other here on LinkedIn.

If I can support you in your professional endeavors, please don't hesitate to reach out!

Sending my best!

{{*your_name*}}

Connection Request Message Fraternity/Sorority 2:

Hi {{*first_name*}} - I am also a {{*fraternity/sorority name*}}! I love connecting with my extended family! Let's add each other here on LinkedIn.

If I can ever do anything to support you in your professional endeavors, please don't hesitate to reach out!

Sending my best!

{{*your_name*}}

Connection Request Message Fraternity/Sorority 3:

Hello my fellow {{*fraternity/sorority*}} {{*brother/ sister*}}!

I thought I'd reach out and say hi. I love connecting with fellow alumni! Let's add each other here on LinkedIn.

If I can ever support you in your professional endeavors, please don't hesitate to reach out!

Sending my best!

{{*your_name*}}

Connection Request Message Fraternity/Sorority 4:

Hi {{*first_name*}} - I noticed you are also a part of

{{*fraternity/sorority*}}! I love connecting with fellow alumni! Let's add each other here on LinkedIn.

If I can ever support you in your professional endeavors, please don't hesitate to reach out!

Sending my best!

{{*your_name*}}

Connection Request Message Fraternity/Sorority 5:

Hi {{*first_name*}} - Looks like you are a fellow {{*fraternity/sorority*}} alumni! Let's connect!

Do any of my contacts stand out to you? I'm happy to make introductions if they would help you grow your career.

Sending my best!

{{*your_name*}}

Connection Request Message Fraternity/Sorority 6:

Hi {{*first_name*}} - Happy {{*today*}} to my fellow {{*fraternity/sorority*}} alumni! I'd love to add you to my network here on LinkedIn.

If any of my contacts can ever be of service to you, please let me know. I'll be happy to make the introduction.

Sending my best!

{{*your_name*}}

Connection Request Message Fraternity/Sorority 7:

Hi {{*first_name*}} - Looks like you are a fellow {{*fraternity/sorority*}} alumni! Let's connect!

If any of my contacts ever stand out as someone you'd like to connect with, please let me know. I'll be happy to make the introduction.

Sending my best!

{{*your_name*}}

Connection Request Message Fraternity/Sorority 8:

Hi {{*first_name*}} - {{*fraternity/sorority*}}! I pledged in {{*year*}}. How long have you been a part of the family? I'd love to add each other here on LinkedIn.

If any of my contacts can ever be of service to you, please let me know. I'll be happy to make the introduction.

Sending my best!

{{*your_name*}}

Connection Request Message Fraternity/Sorority 9:

Hi {{*first_name*}} - Love running into a fellow {{*fraternity/sorority*}} {{*brother/sister*}}! Let's connect here on LinkedIn!

Any connection of mine you might find helpful to your network, please don't hesitate to reach out!

Sending my Best,

{{your_name}}

Connection Request Message Fraternity/Sorority 10:

Hi *{{first_name}}* - Always good to see a *{{fraternity/ sorority}}* *{{brother/sister}}* here on LinkedIn. Let's connect!

If any of my contacts can ever be of service to you, please let me know. I'll be happy to make an introduction.

Sending my best!

{{your_name}}

CONNECTION REQUEST SCRIPTS, RECRUITING

Connection Request Recruiting 1:

Great to virtually meet you. I came across your background on LinkedIn and was really impressed!

Quick question - We are hiring a {{*position*}} here at {{*company*}}! Amazing {{*benefits*}}.

Would this be a good fit for anyone you know?

Please let me know and/or feel free to pass this to anyone that comes to mind.

Thank you in advance for your time to review this, {{*your_name*}}

Connection Request Recruiting 2:

Hi {{*first_name*}} - I'm impressed with your experience at {{*company*}} and wanted to reach out!

I'm not sure if it's for you, but would you happen to know someone who is interested in {{*position*}} at a great company that offers {{*benefits*}}?

Please let me know if you or anyone you know comes to mind.

Thanks!

{{*your_name*}}

Connection Request Recruiting 3:

Hi {{*first_name*}} - I'm impressed with your experience at {{*company*}} and wanted to reach out!

I'm not sure if it's for you, but would you happen to know someone who is interested in {{*position*}} at a great company that offers {{*benefits*}}?

Please let me know if you or anyone you know comes to mind.

Thanks!
{{*your_name*}}

Connection Request Recruiting 4:

Hi {{*first_name*}} - I'm {{*sender.first_name*}} the {{*sender.title*}} over at {{*org.name*}}. I am really impressed with your experience at {{*company*}} and wanted to reach out!

We'd love to talk to you about {{*open position*}} at a great company that offers {{*benefits*}}.

Please let me know if you have time to meet this week.

Thanks!
{{*your_name*}}

Connection Request Recruiting 5:

Hi {{*first_name*}} - I'm {{*first_name*}} the {{*sender. title*}} over at {{*org.name*}}. We would love to talk to you more about a {{*position*}} opening. I can tell you'd be a great fit.

Please let me know if you have time to meet this week.

Thanks!
{{*your_name*}}

Connection Request Recruiting 6:

Hi {{*first_name*}} - I came across your profile earlier this week and had to reach out.

I'd love to talk to you more about {{*position*}} at a great company that offers {{*benefits*}}. You'd be a great addition to the team.

Please let me know if you have time to meet this week.

Thanks!

{{your_name}}

Connection Request Recruiting 7:

Hi *{{first_name}}* - I am the *{{sender.title}}* for *{{org. name}}* and would love to speak with you about joining us in the *{{position}}* at a great company that offers *{{benefits}}*.

Please let me know if you have time to meet this week.

Thanks!

{{your_name}}

Connection Request Recruiting 8:

Hi *{{first_name}}* - *{{sender.first_name}}* over at *{{org. name}}*. *{{Mutual connection}}* recommended you for our new opening as a *{{position}}*.

We'd love to talk to you more about it.

Please let me know if you have time to meet this week.

Thanks!

{{*your_name*}}

Connection Request Recruiting 9:

Hi {{*first_name*}} - I'm{{*sender.first_name*}}, the{{*sender. title*}} with {{*org.name*}}. I noticed your experience with {{*company*}} and would love to talk to you about possible future collaborations.

We have a position open right now that you'd be perfect for. Please let me know if you have time to meet this week.

Thanks!

{{*your_name*}}

Connection Request
Recruiting 10:

Hi {{*first_name*}} - I am reaching out on behalf of {{*org. name*}}. We are so impressed with your experience at {{*company*}} and would love to talk to you about {{*position*}} that recently opened up.

Please let me know if you have time to meet this week. We look forward to learning more about you and hopefully making you an official part of the team.

Thanks!

{{*your_name*}}

CONNECTION REQUEST SCRIPTS, MEETING CALLBACK

Connection Request MTG Callback 1:

Hi {{*first_name*}} - Great speaking with you today and look forward to the opportunity to collaborate.

In the meantime, I'd like to add you to my network on LinkedIn.

If any of my connections can ever help you out in any way, please let me know and I'll be more than happy to make introductions.

Best,

{{*your_name*}}

Connection Request
MTG Callback 2:

Hi {{*first_name*}} - I had a great time speaking with you today and look forward to the opportunity to work together to accomplish {{*goal*}}.

In the meantime, I thought we could stay in touch on LinkedIn.

If any of my connections can ever help you out in any way, please let me know and I'll be more than happy to make introductions.

Best,

{{*your_name*}}

Connection Request
MTG Callback 3:

{{*first_name*}} - I am really looking forward to future collaborations. Today's meeting set a great pace to accomplish {{*goal*}}.

Let's get connected here, that way we can strengthen our mutual connections. Always happy to make an introduction where it might be useful to you.

Best,

{{*your_name*}}

Connection Request
MTG Callback 4:

Hi {{*first_name*}} - So great to meet with you today. I can tell we are going to work really well together in the future.

I'd love to stay connected here on LinkedIn.

If you notice that any of my connections may be helpful to you, please let me know and I'll be more than happy to make introductions.

Best,

{{*your_name*}}

Connection Request
MTG Callback 5:

Hi {{*first_name*}} - I really enjoyed our meeting today about {{*topic/product/collaboration*}}. I look forward to working together on that in the future.

I want to add you to my network here on LinkedIn.

If you come across any connections in my network who stand out, I'm happy to make an introduction for you.

Best,

{{*your_name*}}

Connection Request
MTG Callback 6:

Hi {{*first_name*}} - Today's meeting made me feel so excited about our future collaborations together. I can't wait to accomplish {{*goal*}} with you.

I'd like to add you to my network on LinkedIn.

If there is anything I or someone I am connected to could help you achieve, please don't hesitate to reach out.

Best, {{*your_name*}}

Connection Request
MTG Callback 7:

Hi {{*first_name*}} - I am so impressed by you and your team. I really look forward to collaborating with you on {{*project/service/opportunity*}}.

I'd love to have you become a part of my network on LinkedIn. Let's connect!

My network and I are always here to leverage when you need us.

Best,

{{*your_name*}}

Connection Request
MTG Callback 8:

Hi {{*first_name*}} - It was great speaking with you today and look forward to the opportunity to collaborate.

In the meantime, I'd like to add you to my network on LinkedIn.

If any of my connections can ever help you out in any way, please let me know and I'll be more than happy to make introductions.

Best,

{{*your_name*}}

Connection Request
MTG Callback 9:

{{*first_name*}} - I had such a good time meeting with you today. I can tell that working together is going to be a lot of fun.

I wanted to make sure I added you to my network on LinkedIn.

If any of my connections can ever help you out in any way, please let me know. I'd love to make an introduction I can to help you succeed.

Best,

{{*your_name*}}

Connection Request MTG Callback 10:

Hi {{*first_name*}} - I am so happy with the results of our conversation today. I really look forward to this collaboration and helping you accomplish {{*goal*}}.

That being said, let me know how I can help you leverage my personal network in ways that best suit your needs.

Best,

{{*your_name*}}

CONNECTION REQUEST SCRIPTS, MEETING, THANK YOU AND NEXT STEPS

Connection Request MTG TY + Next Steps 1:

Great meeting you and I look forward to the opportunity to work together. Let's make sure we {{*step 1, 2*}} before meeting again.

In the meantime, I'd like to add you to my network on LinkedIn.

If any of my connections can ever help you out in any way, please let me know and I'll be more than happy to make introductions.

Best,

{{*your_name*}}

Connection Request
MTG TY + Next Steps 2:

Great meeting you!

Let's be sure to {{*step 1, 2*}} before {{*deadline*}}.

Also, I'd love to add you to my network here on LinkedIn.

If any of my connections can ever help you out in any way, please let me know and I'll be more than happy to make introductions.

Best,

{{*your_name*}}

Connection Request
MTG TY + Next Steps 3:

Hi {{*first_name*}} - Great speaking with you today and look forward to the opportunity to collaborate.

Let me know once you have {{*step 1, 2*}}.

In the meantime, I'd like to add you to my network on LinkedIn and make introductions to anyone you might find useful to your career.

Best,

{{your_name}}

Connection Request
MTG TY + Next Steps 4:

Hi *{{first_name}}* - I am so excited about the opportunity to collaborate with you. I really enjoyed our meeting today. Let me know once you have *{{step 1, 2}}*.

Before I see you next, I'd love to add you to my network on LinkedIn and connect you with *{{LinkedIn connection}}*.

It's always nice to be able to share a large network of experts in *{{industry}}*.

Best,

{{your_name}}

Connection Request
MTG TY + Next Steps 5:

Hi {{*first_name*}} - Thank you so much for your time today. I really look forward to our future collaborations. Let me know once you have

{{*step 1, 2*}}.

I'd love to add you to my network on LinkedIn.

If any of my connections look like they can help you out in any way, please let me know and I'll be more than happy to make introductions.

Excited for the possibilities!

Best,

{{*your_name*}}

Connection Request
MTG TY + Next Steps 6:

{{*first_name*}} - Such a great meeting today! I really look forward to working together. I feel committed to doing whatever I can to help you achieve your goals with {{*goal*}}. Let me know once you have {{*step 1, 2*}}.

Best,

{{*your_name*}}

Connection Request
MTG TY + Next Steps 7:

Hi {{*first_name*}} - I am so excited about the opportunity to collaborate with you. I really enjoyed our meeting today. Let me know once you have {{*step 1, 2*}}.

Before I see you next, I'd love to add you to my network on LinkedIn.

Please reach out if you have any questions or see someone you might want an introduction to in my network!

Best,

{{*your_name*}}

Connection Request
MTG TY + Next Steps 8:

Hi {{*first_name*}} - I am so excited for the opportunity to collaborate with you on {{*project/ opportunity/service*}}.

I feel like our meeting went really well today and I can't wait to support you further on {{*goal*}}. Let me know once you have {{*step 1, 2*}}.

In the meantime, we will connect here. Let me know if anyone in my network could be a valuable connection for you.

Best,

{{*your_name*}}

Connection Request
MTG TY + Next Steps 9:

Hi {{*first_name*}} - Awesome meeting today. Thanks for sitting down with me. I think we got a lot covered. I am so excited to take the next steps and help you achieve {{*goal*}}. Let me know once you have {{*step 1, 2*}}.

Before I see you next, I'd love to add you to my network on LinkedIn.

Please let me know if any of my connections look like they can help you out. I'd be more than happy to make introductions.

Best,

{{*your_name*}}

Connection Request
MTG TY + Next Steps 10:

Hi {{*first_name*}} - I am so honored to be moving forward with you in this collaboration. Thank you for your time today. Let me know once you have

{{*step 1, 2*}}.

Before our next meeting, I'd love to add you to my network on LinkedIn. My connections are your connections.

Excited for the future!

Best,

{{*your_name*}}

CONNECTION REQUEST SCRIPTS, POST MEETING

Connection Request Post MTG 1:

{{*first_name*}} - It was so great to meet you! Thank you for taking the time to sit down with me today.

I'd like to add you to my network on LinkedIn.

If any of my connections can ever help you out in any way, please let me know and I'll be more than happy to make introductions.

Best,

{{*your_name*}}

Connection Request
Post MTG 2:

{{*first_name*}} - It was so great to meet you! Thank you for taking the time to sit down with me today.

I'd like to add you to my network on LinkedIn.

If any of my connections can ever help you out in any way, please let me know and I'll be more than happy to make introductions.

Best,

{{*your_name*}}

Connection Request
Post MTG 3:

{{*first_name*}} - It was such an honor to spend time with you today. I hope we can do it again soon to talk about accomplishing {{*goal*}}.

I'd love to add you to my network on LinkedIn.

If any of my connections can ever help you out in any way, please let me know and I'll be more than happy to make introductions.

Best,

{{*your_name*}}

Connection Request Post MTG 4:

{{*first_name*}} - I am so happy I got to meet with you today! Thank you for your time. I learned a lot.

I'd like to add you to my network on LinkedIn.

If any of my connections can ever help you out in any way, please let me know and I'll be more than happy to make introductions.

Best,

{{*your_name*}}

Connection Request
Post MTG 5:

{{*first_name*}} - It was so great to meet you! Thank you for taking the time to sit down with me today. Can't wait to stay in the loop with all you're doing in {{*industry*}}.

I'd love to connect with you here on LinkedIn.

If any connections I have could help propel your growth, I'm happy to make those introductions.

Best,

{{*your_name*}}

Connection Request
Post MTG 6:

{{*first_name*}} - Thank you so much for taking time out of your day to meet with me. I am so impressed by {{*personal compliment*}}.

I'd like to add you to my network on LinkedIn so I can share my network with you if you ever need it. Always happy to help.

Best,

{{*your_name*}}

Connection Request Post MTG 7:

{{*first_name*}} - What a great meeting! Thank you for your time today. I'm so glad I was able to learn more about {{*goal*}}.

Let's connect here on LinkedIn.

If any of my connections look like they can be of service to you, please let me know and I'll be more than happy to make introductions.

Best,

{{*your_name*}}

Connection Request Post MTG 8:

Hi {{*first_name*}} - I am so happy about our meeting today! I'm so glad I got to connect with you and your team in person. It was great to learn more about {{*goal*}}.

Let's add each other here on LinkedIn.

That way, if any of my connections look like they can help you out, I can make an introduction :)

Best,

{{*your_name*}}

Connection Request Post MTG 9:

{{*first_name*}} - I loved being able to sit down with you today to discuss our equal passion for {{*industry topic*}}. Thank you for meeting with me!

Let's stay in touch via LinkedIn. I have a feeling it would be mutually beneficial to tap into one another's network.

Best,

{{*your_name*}}

Connection Request Post MTG 10:

{{*first_name*}} - I had such a good time getting to know you today. I am so impressed by {{*company*}}.

I'd love to add you to my network on LinkedIn.

If any of my connections can ever help you out in any way, please let me know and I'll be more than happy to make introductions.

Best,

{{*your_name*}}

NEW CONNECTION MESSAGE SCRIPTS, THANK YOU

New Connection TY 1:

Hi {{*first_name*}} - I hope you enjoyed the holidays.

I wanted to thank you for recently connecting with me on LinkedIn. I also wanted to make sure you got access to {{*product/service*}}.

I'm looking to help more of my connections and I think you could benefit from using it, here's the link to check it out {{*product link*}}.

Looking forward to keeping in touch.

{{*your_name*}}

New Connection TY 2:

Hey {{*first_name*}} - Thanks for the invite to connect!
Love the LinkedIn content you post here!

If you ever think there is something I can help you out with, please feel free to reach out anytime!

{{*your_name*}}

New Connection TY 3:

Hey {{*first_name*}} - Thanks for the invite to connect! Love the LinkedIn content you post here!

If you ever think there is something I can ever help you out with, please feel free to reach out anytime!

{{*your_name*}}

New Connection TY 4:

Hey {{*first_name*}} - Thanks for connecting with me here on LinkedIn! I value all the content you are posting out here on the platform.

I look forward to the opportunity to collaborate more here and if there is anyone in my network that can ever help you out in any way, please let me know! Happy to make introductions.

My Best,

{{*your_name*}}

New Connection TY 5:

Hey {{*first_name*}} - Thanks for reaching out and connecting with me here on LinkedIn!

I know we have similar interests and mutual connections so I'm excited to learn from you more, network and explore how we can collaborate to maximize each others' success.

If there is anyone in my network that can ever help you out in any way, just let me know I'm happy to make introductions anytime.

My Best,

{{*your_name*}}

New Connection TY 6:

Hey {{*first_name*}} - Great to meet you and thank you for reaching out to connect here on LinkedIn.

If I can ever help you out in any way or have anyone in my network that can take you from Point A to Point B to maximize your success, please don't hesitate to let me know.

All the Best,
{{*your_name*}}

New Connection TY 7:

Hey {{*first_name*}} - Great to meet you and thank you for reaching out to connect here on LinkedIn.

If I can ever help you out in any way, just let me know. Here to support your success anytime.

All the Best,
{{*your_name*}}

New Connection TY 8:

Hi {{*first_name*}} - Thanks for reaching out to connect here on LinkedIn!

I enjoy reading your content and I am here as a resource to help you maximize your success.

Please don't hesitate to reach out anytime!

Here are a few resources that I think you may find of value and apply over the next few weeks:

{{sender.company.asset 1}}

{{sender.company.asset 2}}

{{sender.company.asset 3}}

{{sender.company.asset 4}}

{{sender.company.asset 5}}

All the best,
{{your_name}}

New Connection TY 9:

Hi *{{first_name}}* - Thanks for reaching out and inviting me to connect with you here on LinkedIn.

What can I help you with today?

What are you working on and how can I help you get from here to there to help maximize your success?

Best,

{{*your_name*}}

Message New Connection TY 10:

Hi {{*first_name*}} - Thanks for reaching out and connecting with me here on LinkedIn.

What can I help you with today?

Best,

{{*your_name*}}

INTRODUCTION REQUEST SCRIPTS

Introduction Request 1:

Hi {{*first_name*}} - I wanted to thank you for being such a big part of my professional growth and development over the years. With that, I would love it if you could introduce me to {{*referral name*}}. Your recommendation would go a long way for me.

I've been researching {{*company*}} and would really like to share a few strategies to help them {{*sender value proposition 1*}} and {{*sender value proposition 2*}} and without {{*sender pain 1*}}.

I've also created an introduction template for you to make things as seamless as possible:

Hi {{*first_name*}} - I was just talking to {{*sender_name*}} and think you two should connect. He/she helps companies {{*sender value proposition 1*}} and {{*sender value proposition 2*}}.

This could be a great connection for you both. With that, I will let you two take it from here!

Introduction Request 2:

Hey {{*first_name*}} - Looks like you are doing great! Loved your latest post on {{*topic*}}.

Quick favor... would you mind providing an intro for me to {{*referral name*}}? I noticed you are connected to them and I'd love to chat with them about a big opportunity we have here at

{{*company*}}.

Here is a template you can use if you prefer, to make sending the intro as easy and as fast as possible for you:

Hey - I wanted to connect you with a good friend of mine, {{sender.first_name}} at {{company}}.

They are doing big things in {{industry}} and I know you both have similar passions and interests, so I thought it would be beneficial to connect you two.

I'll let you guys take it from here and wish you both all the best.

Regards,
{{your_name}}

Introduction Request 3:

Hi {{first_name}} - I hope this message finds you well.

I have a quick favor to ask of you. Would you please introduce me to {{referral_name}}? I noticed you are connected to them and I'd love to sit down and talk with them about {{opportunity/topic}}.

I thought I would provide a template for you to make sending the intro as easy and as fast as possible:

Hey {{*first_name*}} - I would love to connect you with a good friend of mine, {{*sender.first_name*}} at {{*company*}}.

They are the {{*sender.title*}} at {{*company*}} and I know the two of you would both benefit from getting to know each other.

I'll let you guys take it from here and wish you both all the best.

Regards,

{{*your_name*}}

Introduction Request 4:

Hey {{*first_name*}} - Really impressed what you have been doing over at {{*company*}}.

I wanted to reach out to ask if you would provide an intro for me to {{*referral_name*}}. I noticed you are connected to them and I'd love to spend some time with them to learn more about {{*topic*}}.

I put together a template you can use to make sending the intro as easy and as fast as possible for you:

Hey - I hope you don't mind if I connect you with a good friend of mine, {{*your_ name*}} at {{*company*}}.

They are doing big things in {{*industry*}} and I know you both have similar passions and interests, so I thought this would be a very beneficial connection.

I'll let you guys take it from here and wish you both all the best.

Regards,
{{*your_name*}}

Introduction Request 5:

Hi {{*first_name*}} - I am reaching out to see if you wouldn't mind helping me with a quick introduction.

I noticed you are connected to {{*referral name*}}.

I've been doing a lot of work with companies like {{*company*}}, and want to share a few strategies to help them {{*sender value proposition 1*}} and {{*sender value proposition 2*}} and without {{*pain 1*}}.

To help make this as easy as possible, I've created a template. You can choose to use and add to it if you wish, or write your own. Whatever you feel more comfortable with.

Thank you so much!
{{*your_name*}}

Template:

Hi {{*first_name*}} - I was just talking to {{*sender.name*}} and think you two should connect. They help companies

{{*sender value proposition 1*}} and {{*sender value proposition 2*}}.

I think they could really help you and wanted to connect you both. With that, I will let you two take it from here!

Introduction Request 6:

Hey {{*first_name*}} - Loved seeing you the other day at {{*event/place*}}! Congrats on {{*latest news*}}.

Hey, I noticed you are connected to {{*referral_ name*}} and I'd love to chat with them about a big opportunity we have here at {{*company*}}. Would you please provide an intro for me? I'd love for my reaching out to feel as organic as possible.

Here is a template you can use if you like, to make sending the intro as easy and as fast as possible for you:

Hey - I wanted to connect you with a good friend of mine, {{*your_name*}} at {{*company*}}.

They would love to set up a time to meet with you.

I know you both have similar passions and interests, so I thought it would be beneficial to connect you two.

I'll let you guys take it from here and wish you both all the best.

Regards,
{{*your_name*}}

Introduction Request 7:

Hey {{*first_name*}} - I wanted to send a quick message to say thank you for introducing me to

{{*referral name*}}. Things are going really well!

I noticed you are also connected to {{*referral_name*}} and I'd love to talk with them as well. Would you please provide another intro for me? I love how organic it feels when you help connect me with people in your network.

Here is another template you can use if you like, to make sending the intro as easy and as fast as possible for you:

Hey, hope all is well!

I wanted to connect you with a good friend of mine,

{{*sender.first_name*}} at {{*company*}}.

They would love to set up a time to meet with you. I know you both experts in your field and would only make sense to get you connected.

250   Sponsored by Seamless.AI, The World's Best Sales Leads. Join for Free at www.seamless.ai

I'll let you guys take it from here and wish you both all the best.

Regards,

{{*your_name*}}

Introduction Request 8:

Hey {{*first_name*}} - Loved seeing you the other day at {{*event/place*}}! Congrats on {{*latest news*}}.

I noticed you are connected to {{*referral name*}} and I'd love to chat with them about a big opportunity we have here at {{*company*}}.

Would you please provide an intro for me? I'd love for my reaching out to feel as organic as possible.

Here is a template you can use if you like, to make sending the intro as easy and as fast as possible for you:

Hey there - I wanted to connect you with a connection of mine, {{*sender.first_name*}} at {{*company*}}.

They would love to set up a time to meet with you.

I know you both have similar passions and interests, so I thought it would be beneficial to connect you two.

I'll let you guys take it from here and wish you both all the best.

Regards,
{{your_name}}

Introduction Request 9:

Hey {{first_name}} - Happy {{today}}!

I noticed you are connected to {{referral name}}. I'd really love an introduction. Would you please provide one for me? I'd love for my reaching out to them to feel as organic as possible.

People ask me what to say all the time so I just created this template if this makes it any easier to do!

Hey - I wanted to connect you with a good friend in my network, {{sender. first_name}} at {{company}}.

They would love to set up a time to meet with you, and based on what I've seen and heard, I know you both could bring a lot of value to one another.

I'll let you guys take it from here and wish you both all the best.

Regards,
{{*your_name*}}

Introduction Request 10:

Hey {{*first_name*}} - So great to speak to you the other day. After our conversation, I noticed that you are connected to {{*referral name*}}. I'd really love to meet them. Would you mind making the introduction? I'd love for my reaching out to them to feel as organic as possible.

Here is a template you can use if you like, to make things simple:

Hey there! Hope all is well.

I wanted to brighten your day by introducing you to,

{{*sender.first_name*}} at {{*company*}}.

They saw your work and would love to set up a time to meet with you. I can say with 100% certainty, this is one connection you will thank me for later ;)

I'll let you guys take it from here and wish you both all the best.

Regards,

{{*your_name*}}

INBOUND LEAD SCRIPTS

Inbound Lead 1:

{{*first_name*}} - Thank you so much for your inquiry about {{*product/service/company*}}. I'd love to set up a phone call with you in the next couple of days to begin the next steps.

Please feel free to reach out to me more directly here:

{{*sender.email*}}

{{*sender.phone_number*}}

Let me know a few times that work best for you. This should only take about {{*time*}}.

Sending my best and looking forward to the future!
{{*your_name*}}

Inbound Lead 2:

{{*first_name*}} - Thank you so much for reaching out about {{*product/service/company*}}. Let's set up a phone call together in the next couple of days to talk about next steps!

You can contact me more directly here:

{{*sender.email*}}

{{*sender.phone_number*}}

Let me know a few times that work best for you. This should only take about {{*time*}}.

Sending my best and looking forward to the future!
{{*your_name*}}

Inbound Lead 3:

{{first_name}} - Thank you so much for your interest in *{{product/service/company}}*. I'd love to get on the phone with you sometime this week to start discussing how to best implement this for you and your team.

Please feel free to reach out to me more directly here:

{{sender.email}}

{{sender.phone_number}}

This should only take about *{{time}}*. Let's find a time that works best for you.

Sending my best and looking forward to the future!
{{your_name}}

Inbound Lead 4:

{{first_name}} - So glad you are interested in *{{product/service/company}}*. Let's set up a phone call to go over what it looks like to work together.

Please feel free to reach out to me more directly here:

{{*sender.email*}}

{{*sender.phone_number*}}

Provide a few times that work best for you. This should only take about {{*time*}}.

Sending my best and looking forward to the future!
{{*your_name*}}

Inbound Lead 5:

{{*first_name*}} - Hope this message finds you well! Thank you for your interest in {{*product/service/ company*}}. Let's find time to get on the phone and discuss your situation at greater length.

Feel free to reach out to me more directly here:

{{*sender.email*}}

{{*sender.phone_number*}}

Provide me with a few times that work best for you and I will accommodate your schedule. Is there anyone else who would likely join this call?

This should only take about {{*time*}}.

Sending my best and looking forward to the future! {{*your_name*}}

Inbound Lead 6:

Hi {{*first_name*}} - So glad you'd like to know more about {{*product/service/company*}}. Let's get on the phone in the next couple of days so we can determine the next steps.

Please feel free to reach out to me more directly here:

{{*sender.email*}}

{{*sender.phone_number*}}

Let me know a few times that work best for you. This should only take about {{*time*}}.

Sending my best and looking forward to the future!

{{your_name}}

Inbound Lead 7:

{{first_name}} - I can't wait to tell you more about

{{product/service/company}}. Thank you for your interest. I'd love to set up a phone call with you in the next couple of days to begin the next steps.

To coordinate times for our follow-up meeting, please contact me directly using the information below:

{{sender.email}}

{{sender.phone_number}}

This should only take about {{time}}. Looking forward to the future!

{{your_name}}

Inbound Lead 8:

Hi {{*first_name*}} - Hope this message finds you well!

I am so excited to walk you through the features and benefits of {{*product/service/company*}}. Let's set up a phone call with you in the next couple of days so we can determine the best route for you!

Please feel free to reach out to me more directly here:

{{*sender.email*}}

{{*sender.phone_number*}}

Send me a few times that work best for you. This should only take about {{*time*}}.

Looking forward to the possibilities! {{*your_name*}}

Inbound Lead 9:

Hi {{*first_name*}} - Excited for you to learn more about {{*product/service/company*}}. I'd love to set up a phone call with you in the next couple of days to give a further overview and figure out the best way to implement this for you and your team.

You can reach out to me more directly here:

{{*sender.email*}}

{{*sender.phone_number*}}

Provide me with a few times that work best for you. This should only take about {{*time*}}.

Looking forward to hearing from you.

{{*your_name*}}

Inbound Lead 10:

{{*first_name*}} - Thank you so much for inquiring about {{*product/service/company*}}! Let's set up a phone call together so I can get a better feel for where you are and how we can best serve you.

Send me a few times that work best for you and I'll give you a call this week. This will only take about {{*time*}}.

{{*sender.email*}}

{{*sender.phone_number*}}

Have a great day! {{*your_name*}}

MESSAGE SCRIPTS
JOB CHANGE

Message - Job Change 1:

Hi {{*first_name*}} - I just wanted to personally congratulate you on the new job you took at {{*company*}}!

They are so lucky to have you over there.

I wish you all the best at the new gig and reach out anytime if you think I or my network can help you out in any way.

All the best,

{{*first_name*}}

Message - Job Change 2:

Hi {{*first_name*}} - I noticed you just took the {{*position*}} role at {{*company*}}! Congratulations. They are so fortunate to have you over there.

Keep me posted on how things are going and as always, let me know how I can help in any way!

All the best, {{*first_name*}}

Message - Job Change 3:

Hi {{*first_name*}} - Wow, congratulations!!! I just saw you took a new position over there at {{*company*}}!

They are so lucky to have you. I'm excited to see the impact you make.

If I can ever help you maximize your success at{{*company*}}, just let me know anytime. My direct line is {{*sender.phone_number*}}.

Best,

{{your_name}}

Message - Job Change 4:

{{first_name}} - Just heard the good news about your move to *{{company}}*. Congrats!

You're probably neck-deep in getting acclimated to your new environment.

When you come up for air next week or two, let's grab lunch. Good luck and talk soon!

Cheers,

{{your_name}}

Message - Job Change 5:

Hey *{{first_name}}* - I just saw the news about your new gig at *{{company}}*! Wow, that is amazing!!!

They are so lucky to have you, I'm excited to see the impact you make.

If I can ever help you maximize your success at

{{*company*}}, just let me know. My direct line is {{*sender. phone_number*}}

Good luck,
{{*your_name*}}

Message - Job Change 6:

Hey {{*first_name*}} - I just heard the news about your new gig at {{*company*}}! Wow, congratulations!!!

I'm sure they will love having you there. I'm excited to see the impact you make.

If I can ever help you maximize your success at

{{*company*}}, just let me know anytime my direct line is {{*sender.phone_number*}} or shoot me an email at {{*sender.email*}}

Cheers to your biggest and best year yet ahead!
{{*your_name*}}

Message - Job Change 7:

Congratulations on your new job at {{company}}! Simply amazing, they are so lucky to have you!

If I can ever help you maximize your success at {{company}}, just let me know any time... my direct line is {{sender.phone_number}} or {{sender.email}}.

All the Best,
{{your_name}}

Message - Job Change 8:

Congratulations on your new job at {{company}}! So happy for you, you are going to crush it and {{new company}} is so lucky to have you over there!

If I can ever help you maximize your success at {{new company}}, let me know at any time.

My direct line is {{sender_phone}} or {{sender_email}}.

All the Best,

{{your_name}}

Message - Job Change 9:

Congrats on your latest progress in starting *{{new job}}*. I'm excited for you and admire the bold life changes!

I know you're probably in the midst of many decisions, but if *{{company}}* and I can be helpful in any way, please let me know!

Keep me posted on how the transition is coming, and I look forward to hearing from you soon.

Best of luck to you,

{{your_name}}

Message - Job Change 10:

{{first_name}} - Just saw you made some big career changes - Congrats!

It seems like you're in a much bigger and lucrative industry than before.

When you get settled, I'd love to find a good time for a call and learn about the new company. I know our {{*product/service*}} helped you increase deal flow before, and if you think we'd be a good fit at {{*company*}}, let us know and we will help any way we can.

Talk with you soon and definitely check out how we closed {{*client case study*}}. From one sales guy to another, you'll appreciate the stat.

Cheers,

{{*your_name*}}

MESSAGE SCRIPTS, PAST COWORKER

Message - Past Coworker 1:

Hi {{*first_name*}} - I noticed you used to work at {{*company*}}! So did I! Small world. Did you ever spend any time in the {{*division*}} division?

Anyway, I love connecting with work alumni, let's add each other here on LI.

Sending my best!
{{*your_name*}}

Message - Past Coworker 2:

Hi {{*first_name*}} - I noticed you also used to work at {{*company*}}! I love connecting with work alumni, let's add each other here on LI.

Best,

{{*your_name*}}

Message - Past Coworker 3:

Hi {{*first_name*}} - Your profile caught my eye because I also used to work for {{*company*}}. It looks like we have a lot of similar experiences.

Let's add each other here on LI. If any of my contacts look like they can help you in any way, don't hesitate to reach out. I'm always happy to make introductions.

Have a great day!

{{*your_name*}}

Message - Past Coworker 4:

Hi {{*first_name*}} - I noticed that you also used to work for {{*company*}} so I thought I would add you here on LI. It looks like we have a lot of similar experiences.

If any of my contacts look like they can help you, let me know and I'll make the introduction!

Keep it touch,

{{*your_name*}}

Message - Past Coworker 5:

Hi {{*first_name*}} - I'd love to add you here on LinkedIn. I noticed you also used to work for {{*company*}}. I had such a great time there! Learned a lot.

Hey, let me know how I can help you connect with other like-minded individuals in our space. More than happy to make that introduction...

All my best!

{{*your_name*}}

Message - Past Coworker 6:

Hi {{*first_name*}} - It looks like we have a lot of similar work experience! I also used to {{*position*}} for {{*company*}}. A lot of my {{*industry*}} experience came from working there.

Let's add each other here on LI. My connections are your connections, and I'm always happy to make introductions where necessary. Just keep that in mind!

Have an awesome week,

{{*your_name*}}

Message - Past Coworker 7:

Hi {{*first_name*}} - I love connecting with people who also used to work for {{*company*}}. Such a great company culture!

Let's add each other here on LI. If any of my contacts look like they can help you in any way, don't hesitate to reach out. I'm always happy to make introductions. Hope this finds you well.

Sending my best!

{{*your_name*}

Message - Past Coworker 8:

Hi {{*first_name*}} - I'm connecting with as many people as I can who also used to work for

{{*company*}}. I figured we could all help support each other as we grow professionally.

Let's add each other here on LI. If any of my contacts look like they can help you in any way, don't hesitate to reach out. I'm always happy to make introductions.

Cheers!

{{*your_name*}}

Message - Past Coworker 9:

Hi {{*first_name*}} - Looks like you used to work for {{*company*}} too! Awesome. I love connecting with work alumni. What was your biggest take away from {{*company*}}? I know I wouldn't be where I am today if it weren't for {{*experience*}}.

Let's add each other here on LI. If any of my contacts look like they can help you in any way, don't hesitate to reach out. I'm always happy to make introductions.

Best,

{{*your_name*}}

Message - Past Coworker 10:

Hi {{*first_name*}} - I thought I'd reach out because

I also used to work for {{*company*}}! It looks like we have a lot of similar experiences.

Let's add each other here on LI. I'd love to support you in any way I can. If any of my contacts look like they can help you in any way, don't hesitate to reach out. I'm always happy to make introductions.

Sending my best!

{{*your_name*}}

MESSAGE SCRIPTS, SCHEDULE MEETING

Message - Schedule Meeting 1:

{{*first_name*}} - I was looking over your profile and what you're doing over at {{*company*}} is really impressive. I would love to find time this week to sit down with you personally to discuss {{*goal*}}.

Let me know your availability.

Have a good one,

{{*your_name*}}

Message - Schedule Meeting 2:

{{*first_name*}} - I noticed that you are also working in the {{*industry*}}. I would love to find time this week to sit down with you personally to discuss {{*opportunity*}}. It would be great to get your insight. Let me know your availability.

Thanks!

{{*your_name*}}

Message - Schedule Meeting 3:

{{*first_name*}} - I am so impressed with your work over at {{*company*}}. I would love to find time this week to sit down with you personally to discuss {{*goal/opportunity/product/idea*}}. I think it is something that could really benefit both of us moving forward.

Let me know a good time for you.

Looking forward to it,

{{*your_name*}}

Message - Schedule Meeting 4:

{{*first_name*}} - I was looking over your profile and what you're doing over at {{*company*}} is really impressive. I would love to find time this week to sit down with you personally to discuss {{*goal*}}.

Let me know your availability.

Thanks!
{{*your_name*}}

Message - Schedule Meeting 5:

{{*first_name*}} - I wanted to reach out personally because I have been following you for some time and I would love to meet with you personally to talk about {{*goal*}}.

Would you be willing to give me {{*time*}} of your time?

I would be so grateful to get to know you better. Let me know what your schedule is like and I will accommodate your needs.

Thank you,

{{your_name}}

Message - Schedule Meeting 6:

{{first_name}} - I just read your latest post about *{{topic}}*.

I am so impressed with your insight into *{{topic/industry}}*. I would love to learn more from you. Would you be open to a *{{time}}* meeting sometime this week?

If so, let me know your availability and I will accommodate your schedule.

Thanks!

{{your_name}}

Message - Schedule Meeting 7:

{{first_name}} - I am really inspired by your recent work with *{{company}}*. I would love to talk to you one-on-one. I love learning from other industry experts and would be so grateful to get thirty minutes of your time.

If this is something you are open to, let me know your availability and I will accommodate your schedule.

Best,

{{*your_name*}}

Message - Schedule Meeting 8:

{{*first_name*}} - I noticed you are also working in {{*industry*}}. We seem to have many similar interests and professional experiences. I would love to meet up sometime to talk to you about

{{*goal*}}. I really enjoy connecting with other industry professionals to gain their insight.

What day/time works best for us to have this conversation?

Much appreciated,

{{*your_name*}}

Message - Schedule Meeting 9:

{{*first_name*}} - I would love to find some time in the near future to meet with you and discuss {{*goal*}}.

I would really value your input and perspective.

Would you be willing to carve out thirty minutes this week?

Let me know your availability.

Thanks!
{{*your_name*}}

Message - Schedule Meeting 10:

Hi {{*first_name*}} - I am meeting with other

{{*industry*}} professionals to learn more about {{*topic*}}. I have noticed your extensive experience in {{*field*}} and would love 30 minutes of your time to learn more about {{*topic*}}. Would you be open to sitting down sometime this week?

Here is a link to my calendar {{*link*}}. Choose a time and let's get together!

Looking forward to it,

{{*your_name*}}

MESSAGE SCRIPTS, MEETING REMINDER

Message - Meeting Reminder 1:

Hi {{*first_name*}} - I wanted to quickly reach out and remind you about our meeting together this {{*day*}} at {{*time*}}.

I look forward to speaking with you more at that time. Have a great day!

See you soon.
{{*your_name*}}

Message - Meeting Reminder 2:

Hi {{*first_name*}} - I wanted to remind you of our meeting together this week. We had set {{*day*}} at {{*time*}}. Does this still work for you? I look forward to speaking with you more at that time.

Have a great day!

See you soon,

{{your_name}}

Message - Meeting Reminder 3:

Hi {{*first_name*}} - I am looking forward to our meeting this week on {{*day*}} at {{*time*}}.
I wanted to reach out to you to confirm.

Look forward to speaking with you.

Have a great day!
{{your_name}}

Message - Meeting Reminder 4:

Hi {{*first_name*}} - I am excited for our meeting together this {{*day*}} at {{*time*}} to discuss {{*goal*}}. Send me a quick message to confirm.

Looking forward to the possibilities. Have a great day!

See you soon.

{{*your_name*}}

Message - Meeting Reminder 5:

Hi {{*first_name*}} - I am confirming our meeting together this {{*day*}} at {{*time*}} to discuss {{*goal*}}.

Looking forward to speaking with you about the possibilities of working together in the near future.

Have a great day!

Talk to you soon,

{{*your_name*}}

Message - Meeting Reminder 6:

Hi {{*first_name*}} - Looking forward to getting together this week.

I have {{*day*}} at {{*time*}} on my calendar. Does this still work for you? Looking forward to the possibilities.

Sending my Best,

{{*your_name*}}

Message - Meeting Reminder 7:

Hi {{*first_name*}} - Reaching out to confirm our meeting this {{*day*}} at {{*time*}} to discuss {{*goal*}}. I am planning to meet you at {{*place*}}.

Please let me know if this is still what works best for you. I am happy to accommodate your schedule.

Looking forward to the possibilities.

See you soon.

{{*your_name*}}

Message - Meeting Reminder 8:

Hi {{*first_name*}} - I am really looking forward to speaking with you this week about {{*goal*}}. I have {{*day*}} at {{*time*}} in my calendar and wanted to confirm quickly with you.

Have a great day! See you soon.

{{*your_name*}}

Message - Meeting Reminder 9:

Dear {{*first_name*}}:

I was thinking about you and thought you would enjoy seeing/reading the following article: {{*link to article*}}.

I think this aligns with what you are trying to accomplish. Let me know if there is anything else I can do to help you.

Once again, my direct phone number is: {{*sender. phone_number*}}. Looking forward to speaking with you next {{*day*}} at {{*time*}}.

Sincerely,

{{*your_name*}}

Message - Meeting Reminder 10:

Hi {{*first_name*}} - Our meeting this week is going to be a game-changer! I have it on my calendar for this {{*day*}} at {{*time*}}. Send me a quick message to confirm. Can't wait to show you more about {{*topic/ goal/product/service*}}.

Looking forward to the possibilities.

Talk soon!

{{*your_name*}}

MESSAGE SCRIPTS, RESCHEDULE MEETING

Message - Reschedule Meeting 1:

Hi {{*first_name*}} - I was really looking forward to speaking with you this week about {{*goal*}}. Unfortunately, I am wondering if we can reschedule to {{*day*}} at {{*time*}}.

Let me know if this works for you. If not, please feel free to suggest a time.

Thank you for understanding,
{{*your_name*}}

Message - Reschedule Meeting 2:

Hi {{*first_name*}} - I am reaching out about the possibility of rescheduling our meeting from {{*day*}} at {{*time*}} to {{*day*}} at {{*time*}}.

If this will not work for you, please feel free to suggest a time. Sorry about that!

Hope to chat soon,

{{*your_name*}}

Message - Reschedule Meeting 3:

Hi {{*first_name*}} - Would you be open to rescheduling our meeting from {{*day*}} at {{*time*}} to {{*day*}} at {{*time*}}? Please feel free to suggest another time if this will not work for you.

Thank you for your flexibility.

Have a great day!

{{*your_name*}}

Message - Reschedule Meeting 4:

Hi {{*first_name*}} - I apologize for having to do this, but do you mind rescheduling our meeting from {{*day*}} at {{*time*}} to {{*day*}} at {{*time*}}?

If this doesn't work let's get on the phone and find a new time ASAP.

{{*sender.phone_number*}}

Have a great day! See you soon.
{{*your_name*}}

Message - Reschedule Meeting 5:

Hi {{*first_name*}} - I regret asking this, but could we reschedule our meeting this week? I want to make sure we both have adequate time to prepare after our conversation yesterday.

May I suggest {{*day*}} at {{*time*}} or {{*day*}} at {{*time*}}?

If these times will not work for you, please feel free to suggest another one. I am happy to accommodate your schedule.

Have a great day!
{{*your_name*}}

Message - Reschedule Meeting 6:

Hi {{*first_name*}} - I am going to need to reschedule our meeting this week if that is okay with you.

I am slammed right now and want to make sure I find a time where I can give you the attention you deserve.

May I suggest {{*day*}} at {{*time*}} or {{*day*}} at {{*time*}}?

If these times will not work for you, please feel free to suggest another one. I am happy to accommodate your schedule.

Thank you for understanding and hope to get this situated ASAP,
{{*your_name*}}

Message - Reschedule Meeting 7:

Hi {{*first_name*}} - Would it be okay if we moved our meeting this week from {{*day*}} at {{*time*}} to {{*day*}} at {{*time*}}? I think we will need to schedule a little more time to cover everything.

If these times will not work for you, please feel free to suggest another one. I am happy to accommodate your schedule.

Have a great day! See you soon.

{{*your_name*}}

Message - Reschedule Meeting 8:

Hi {{*first_name*}} - Can we reschedule our meeting this week? I want to make sure we both have adequate time to prepare after our conversation yesterday.

May I suggest {{*day*}} at {{*time*}} or {{*day*}} at {{*time*}}?

If these times will not work for you, please feel free to suggest another one. I am happy to accommodate your schedule.

See you soon, {{*your_name*}}

Message - Reschedule Meeting 9:

Hi {{*first_name*}},

Would you be willing to reschedule our meeting this week? I want to make sure we find the best time to get together so we don't feel rushed.

Would {{*day*}} at {{*time*}} or {{*day*}} at {{*time*}} work for you?

If not, please feel free to suggest another one. I am happy to accommodate your schedule.

Thank you,
{{*your_name*}}

Message - Reschedule Meeting 10:

Hi {{*first_name*}},

Do you have the flexibility to reschedule our meeting this week?

I would be so appreciative for your patience and am happy to accommodate your schedule.

Here is a link to my calendar {{*sender.calendar_url*}}. Feel free to choose a time that works best for you.

Thank you again,

{{*your_name*}}

MESSAGE SCRIPTS, MEETING CALLBACK

Message Meeting Callback 1:

{{*first_name*}} - Thank you so much for meeting with me on {{*day*}}. I wanted to touch base with you about scheduling a phone call to follow up on our conversation.

Here is a link to my calendar: {{*sender.calendar_url*}}

Please choose a time that works best for you. Look forward to speaking with you again.

Sending my best!

{{*your_name*}}

Message
Meeting Callback 2:

{{*first_name*}} - I am so glad we were able to meet this week. I want to set up a phone call with you to talk about our next steps.

Here is a link to my calendar: {{*sender.calendar_url*}}

Please choose a time that works best for you and I will give you a call. Looking forward to speaking with you again.

Sending my best!

{{*your_name*}}

Message
Meeting Callback 3:

{{*first_name*}} - I am so excited about the outcome of our meeting last {{*day*}}. Let's schedule a phone call to follow up.

Here is a link to my calendar: {{*sender.calendar_url*}}

Please choose a time that works best for you.

Looking forward to working together in the near future.

Sending my best!

{{*your_name*}}

Message
Meeting Callback 4:

{{*first_name*}} - Thank you for sitting down with me to discuss the possibilities of collaborating in the future. Let's get on the phone this week to discuss what's next.

Here is a link to my calendar: {{*sender.calendar_url*}}

Please choose a time that works best for you.

Looking forward to it!

{{*your_name*}}

Message
Meeting Callback 5:

{{*first_name*}} - I hope this message finds you well. I wanted to set up a quick phone call to touch base after our meeting last {{*day*}}.

Here is a link to my calendar: {{*sender.calendar_url*}}

Please choose a time that works best for you.

Looking forward to it,

{{*your_name*}}

Message
Meeting Callback 6:

{{*first_name*}} - Thank you so much for your time yesterday! I'd like to set up a quick {{*time*}} phone call to follow up and get your initial feelings and feedback.

Here is a link to my calendar: {{*sender.calendar_url*}}

Please choose a time that works best for you and I will give you a call. Look forward to speaking with you again.

Thanks again,

{{*your_name*}}

Message
Meeting Callback 7:

{{*first_name*}} - I am so excited to be moving forward with you on {{*goal*}}. Let's touch base over the phone this week and get ready to begin this work together.

Here is a link to my calendar: {{*sender.calendar_url*}}

Please choose a time that works best for you.

Look forward to speaking with you again,

{{*your_name*}}

Message
Meeting Callback 8:

{{*first_name*}} - Happy {{*today*}}!

I'd love to set up a quick follow-up phone call this week to get a sense of how you are feeling after our meeting on {{*day*}}.

Here is a link to my calendar: {{*sender.calendar_url*}}

Please choose a time that works best for you. Look forward to speaking with you again.

Sending my best!
{{*your_name*}}

Message
Meeting Callback 9:

{{*first_name*}} - I'd love to find 15-30 minutes this week to get on the phone with you and get a feel for where things are after our meeting together last week.

Here is a link to my calendar: {{*sender.calendar_url*}}

Go ahead and choose the best time for you!

Look forward to speaking with you again and excited about the possibilities,

{{*your_name*}}

Message
Meeting Callback 10:

{{*first_name*}} - Hope your day is going well! I'd love it if you would take a few moments to choose a time from my calendar link below for a follow-up phone call on our meeting last week.

{{*sender.calendar_url*}}

Choose a time that works best for you. I look forward to speaking with you again.

Have an awesome day,

{{*your_name*}}

MESSAGE SCRIPTS, PROPOSAL, THANK YOU, NEXT STEPS

Message
Proposal, TY, Next Steps 1:

Hi {{*first_name*}} - Thank you so much for taking the time to sit down with me and talk about the possibilities of implementing {{*product/service*}}.

Let me know when you have completed {{*step 1, 2, 3*}}. Looking forward to seeing you again.

My Best,

{{*your_name*}}

Message
Proposal, TY, Next Steps 2:

Hi {{*first_name*}} - I loved being able to talk with you the other day about solving {{*problem*}} *with* {{*product/ service*}}.

Once you have completed {{*step 1, 2, 3*}}, let me know and we'll get on the phone again to discuss what's next.

Looking forward to seeing you again,
{{*your_name*}}

Message
Proposal, TY Next Steps 3:

Hi {{*first_name*}} - Thank you so much for taking the time to sit down with me earlier this week. I'd love to continue our conversation about the implementation of {{*product/service*}}.

Let me know when you have {{*step 1, 2*}} and we'll set up our next meeting.

Looking forward to seeing you again.

Best,

{{your_name}}

Message
Proposal, TY, Next Steps 4:

Hi {{*first_name*}} - I'm so glad we were able to talk about how {{*product/service*}} can best fit your needs.

Let me know when you have completed {{*step 1, 2, 3*}}, then we can set up our next time to meet and continue on with the process.

Looking forward to seeing you again and excited to work together.

Have a great one,

{{your_name}}

Message
Proposal, TY Next Steps 5:

Hi {{*first_name*}} - Thank you for your interest in {{*product/service*}}. As we discussed in our first meeting, after you have {{*step 1, 2, 3*}} we can get on the phone and finalize things in order to move forward.

Feel free to reach out to me at any time with questions. Looking forward to the future!

Cheers,

{{*your_name*}}

Message
Proposal, TY, Next Steps 6:

Hi {{*first_name*}} - It was so good to sit down with you and talk about how {{*product/service*}} can solve {{*problem*}} I am so excited to get you and

{{*company*}} moving on this.

Let me know when you have completed {{*step 1, 2, 3*}} and we will set up our next meeting time to move things forward.

Looking forward to seeing you again.

My Best,
{{*your_name*}}

Message
Proposal, TY, Next Steps 7:

Hi {{*first_name*}} - What a great first meeting! I am so excited I got to share {{*product/service*}} with you and your team.

Let me know if you have any questions completing

{{*step 1, 2, 3*}}. Then we will find a time to sit down together again and talk about what is best for

{{*company*}}.

See you again soon!
{{*your_name*}}

Message Proposal, TY, Next Steps 8:

Hi {{*first_name*}} - I am so glad I was able to show you more about {{*product/service*}} earlier this week. Let me know when you have completed {{*step 1, 2, 3*}} so we can get moving as soon as possible to help {{*company*}} achieve {{*goal*}}.

More than happy to jump on a call to walk you through these.

Have a great day!

{{*your_name*}}

Message Proposal, TY, Next Steps 9:

Hi {{*first_name*}} - It was so good to meet with you about {{*product/service*}}. I am so excited for the potential difference it can make for you and {{*company*}} as you move forward towards {{*goal*}}.

Let's do this. Go ahead and complete {{*step 1, 2, 3*}} and we will get together as soon as you have this completed.

Can't wait to get started,

{{*your_name*}}

Message
Proposal, TY, Next Steps 10:

Hi {{*first_name*}} - What a great first meeting! I am so thrilled to see where {{*product/service*}} can take you and {{*company*}}.

Let me know when you have completed {{*step 1, 2, 3*}}. Let's set another meeting as soon as that is done and get this moving!

Looking forward to seeing you again.

My best,

{{*your_name*}}

MESSAGE SCRIPTS, PROPOSAL CALLBACK

Message - Proposal Callback 1:

{{*first_name*}} - I hope this message finds you well. I wanted to touch base with you and schedule a phone call to follow up on our conversation about {{*product/ solution*}}.

Here is a link to my calendar: {{*sender.calendar_url*}}

Please choose a time that works best for you. Look forward to speaking with you again.

Sending my best!

{{*your_name*}}

Message - Proposal Callback 2:

{{*first_name*}} - Happy {{*today*}}! I'd love to set up a phone call with you to talk about the next steps for {{*product/solution*}}.

Here is a link to my calendar: {{*sender.calendar_url*}}

Go ahead and choose a time that works best for you and I will give you a call.

Look forward to speaking with you again.

Best,
{{*your_name*}}

Message - Proposal Callback 3:

{{*first_name*}} - I am so excited to talk to you more about {{*product/service*}}. Let's schedule a phone call to follow up.

The best way to do that is to choose a time on my calendar here: {{*sender.calendar_url*}}

Please choose a time that works best for you.

Looking forward to working together in the near future.

Sending my best!

{{*your_name*}}

Message - Proposal Callback 4:

{{*first_name*}} - Thank you for sitting down with me to discuss the possibilities of collaborating in the near future. Next, I would love to jump on a call to hash out some of the details of moving forward!

If you could, please choose a link to my calendar, and we will go from there: {{*sender.calendar_url*}}

Looking forward to it!

{{*your_name*}}

Message - Proposal Callback 5:

{{*first_name*}} - I hope this message finds you well. I wanted to set up a quick phone call with you to discuss {{*product/solution*}}.

Here is a link to my calendar: {{*sender.calendar_url*}}

Please choose a time that works best for you and let's get this moving forward!

Sending my Best,
{{*your_name*}}

Message - Proposal Callback 6:

{{*first_name*}} - Thank you so much for your time yesterday! I'd like to set up a quick 15-minute phone call to follow up and get your initial feelings and feedback.

The most convenient way is to grab a time on my calendar here: {{*sender.calendar_url*}}

Whatever you find works best for you, I will give you a call and we will move forward from there.

Looking forward to the next conversation,

{{*your_name*}}

Message - Proposal Callback 7:

{{*first_name*}} - I am so excited to be moving forward with you on {{*goal*}}. Let's touch base over the phone this week and get ready to take the next steps.

Let's link up calendars and see what works for a follow-up: {{*sender. calendar_url*}}

Looking forward to our next conversation.

Best,

{{*your_name*}}

Message - Proposal Callback 8:

{{*first_name*}} - Happy {{*today*}}!

I'd love to set up a quick phone call this week to get your initial feelings on {{*product/solution*}} so we can plan for what is best moving forward.

Here is a link to my calendar: {{*sender.calendar_url*}} - Please choose a time that works best for you.

Look forward to helping you achieve {{*growth goals*}}, {{*your_name*}}

Message - Proposal Callback 9:

{{*first_name*}} - I'd love to find 15-30 minutes this week to get on the phone and discuss your thoughts about {{*product/service*}}.

Here is a link to my calendar: {{*sender.calendar_url*}} - Please share this invite with whoever else you'd like to have in our follow-up!

Please choose a time that works best for you so we can continue the conversation and get a feel for the next steps.

{{*your_name*}}

Message - Proposal Callback 10:

{{*first_name*}} - Hope your day is going well! I'd love it if you could take a few moments to choose a time from my calendar link below to set up a phone call so we can discuss {{*product/service*}} in greater detail.

{{*sender.calendar_url*}}

Look forward to speaking with you.

Sending my best!

{{*your_name*}}

MESSAGE SCRIPTS, NEW CUSTOMER

Message - New Customer 1:

Hi {{*first_name*}} - Welcome to the {{*company*}} family. We are so excited to have you and are grateful you've chosen {{*product/service*}}.

I wanted to personally reach out to thank you and let you know I am here should you need anything.

Please don't hesitate to reach out for any reason.

Sending my best and so glad to have you!
{{*your_name*}}

Message - New Customer 2:

Hi {{*first_name*}} - Thank you for choosing {{*product/ service*}}! We are thrilled to have you and {{*company*}} as a customer and look forward to building a long-term relationship.

Please don't hesitate to reach out if you need anything. I am here to help!

Sending my best and so glad to have you!
{{*your_name*}}

Message - New Customer 3:

Hi {{*first_name*}} - How are you enjoying {{*product/ service*}} so far? We are so glad to have you and can't wait to be a part of helping you {{*goal*}}.

I wanted to personally reach out to thank you. I am always here if you need anything so please don't hesitate to reach out for any reason.

So glad to have you,

{{*your_name*}}

Message - New Customer 4:

Hi {{*first_name*}} - We are so excited to have you as our newest customer and are so grateful you've chosen {{*product/service*}}.

I wanted to personally reach out to you and make sure you know I am here for you if you need anything. Never hesitate to reach out if you need me!

Sending my best and so glad to have you on board,

{{*your_name*}}

Message - New Customer 5:

Hi {{*first_name*}} - Thank you so much for choosing {{*product/service*}}! I am so grateful to be the one to help get you started.

Please don't hesitate to reach out for any reason. Think of me as an extension of your team and support whenever you need me.

Looking forward to helping you have your best year yet,
{{*your_name*}}

Message - New Customer 6:

Hi {{*first_name*}} - Congratulations on becoming the newest member of the {{*company*}} family! We are thrilled you have chosen {{*product/service*}}.

Looking forward to assisting you and sending you my best.

Always here to help,
{{*your_name*}}

Message - New Customer 7:

Hi {{first_name}} - Welcome to {{company}}! I am so excited we have been able to implement and move forward together with {{product/service}}.

I wanted to personally reach out to thank you for your desire and willingness to work together. I can wait to help you {{goal}}.

Please don't hesitate to reach out for any reason. I'm here to help at any time!

Sending my best and so glad to have you!
{{your_name}}

Message - New Customer 8:

Hi {{first_name}} - We are so happy to have you as our newest customer for {{product/service}}. Thank you for trusting us to help you {{goal}}!

Just so you know, I'm personally here to help anytime you ever need anything from us.

Please don't hesitate to reach out for any reason.

Cheers,

{{*your_name*}}

Message - New Customer 9:

Hi {{*first_name*}} - Congrats on getting started with {{*product/service*}}. I know it is going to radically improve your ability to {{*goal*}}.

I wanted to personally reach out to thank you for your business. Please don't hesitate to reach out for any reason. I am here to help in any way I can!

Sending my best and so glad to have you!

{{*your_name*}}

Message - New Customer 10:

Wow {{*first_name*}}!

So glad to have you on board with {{*product/ service*}}.

I wanted to personally reach out to thank you for becoming a part of the {{*company*}} community. I will be your point of contact moving forward, so please reach out anytime you need me!

Happy to have you,

{{*your_name*}}

MESSAGE SCRIPTS, CUSTOMER CHECK-IN

Message - Customer Check-In 1:

{{*first_name*}} - I hope this message finds you well! I wanted to check in with you to see how things are going with {{*product/service*}}.

Please let me know if you have any questions or if I can be of service in any way.

Best, {{*your_name*}}

Message - Customer Check-In 2:

{{*first_name*}} - I wanted to quickly check in with you to see how things are going with {{*product/ service*}}. I'm glad we are on our way to helping you {{*goal*}}!

Please let me know if you have any questions or if I can be of service in any way.

Have a great day!

{{*your_name*}}

Message - Customer Check-In 3:

{{*first_name*}} - Happy {{*today*}}! I am checking in to see how things are going for you and {{*company*}} with {{*product/service*}}.

What's your experience been like so far? We would love to hear from you.

In the meantime, please don't hesitate to reach out if you have any questions.

Keep in touch,

{{*your_name*}}

Message - Customer Check-In 4:

{{*first_name*}} - I hope you are having a great day so far! How are you doing with your newly implemented {{*product/service*}}.

Excited to hear how it's going for you. Let me know how I can be of service!

Have a wonderful day,

{{*your_name*}}

Message - Customer Check-In 5:

{{*first_name*}} - How things are going with

{{*product/service*}}? I wanted to check in to see if there is anything I can do to further support you at this time.

Don't hesitate to contact me here directly.

Enjoy your day,

{{*your_name*}}

Message - Customer Check-In 6:

{{*first_name*}} - I hope this message finds you well! I am touching base to see if there is anything I can do to support you with your newly added {{*product/ service*}}.

What's your experience been like so far?

As always, please let me know if you have any questions or if I can be of service in any way.

Make it a great day,

{{*your_name*}}

Message - Customer Check-In 7:

{{*first_name*}} - Happy {{*today*}}! How is your new {{*product/service*}}? I wanted to check in to make sure everything is going well during these beginning stages.

If you have any questions, please don't hesitate to reach out! Otherwise, here's a link to our {{*Q&A portal*}} for a wide variety of informative materials.

Cheers!

{{*your_name*}}

Message - Customer Check-In 8:

Hi {{*first_name*}} - How are you? Just checking in to see how things are going with {{*product/service*}}.

Please let me know if you have any questions or if I can be of service in any way.

Have a great day!

{{your_name}}

Message - Customer Check-In 9:

{{first_name}} - I hope things are going well for you this week. I wanted to reach out to you personally to see how things are going with {{product/service}}.

What do you see as some of the pros and cons so far?

Let me know what you think, and as always, let me know how I can be of assistance.

Have a wonderful {{today}},

{{your_name}}

Message - Customer Check-In 10:

{{*first_name*}} - I hope this message finds you well. I am checking in with you to make sure things are running smoothly with {{*product/service*}}.

What's your favorite thing about using it so far?

Please let me know if you have any questions or if any of your teammates need us to set them up as well.

Best of luck to you,

{{*your_name*}}

MESSAGE SCRIPTS, CUSTOMER RENEWAL

Message - Customer Renewal 1:

Hi {{*first_name*}} - I wanted to personally reach out to thank you for renewing your {{*contract/ subscription*}} with {{*product/service*}}. We love having you as a customer and are here to help support you in any way we can.

Please let me know if there is anything I can do to help you {{*goal*}}.

Have a great day,

{{*your_name*}}

Message - Customer Renewal 2:

Hi {{*first_name*}} - Thank you for your recent renewal of {{*company's*}} {{*contract/subscription*}} of {{*product/service*}}. We love having you as a customer and are here to help support you in any way we can.

Please let me know if there is anything I can do to help you {{*goal*}}.

Sending my best!
{{*your_name*}}

Message - Customer Renewal 3:

Hi {{*first_name*}} - I am so excited to hear that you are renewing {{*contract/subscription*}} with

{{*product/service*}}. If there is anything you need, please let me know.

Always here to help.

Best,

{{your_name}}

Message - Customer Renewal 4:

Hi *{{first_name}}* - I am so glad you renewed your

{{contract/subscription}} with *{{product/service}}*! We love having you as a customer.

We are so excited to help you with *{{goal}}* and want to let you know we are here to help however we can!

Never hesitate to reach out,

{{your_name}}

Message - Customer Renewal 5:

Hi *{{first_name}}* - Thank you for choosing to continue with *{{product/service}}*!

We love having you as a customer and are honored to be a part of your company's growth and success.

This is my direct line if you are ever in need of assistance with {{*goal*}}.

All my Best,

{{*your_name*}}

Message - Customer Renewal 6:

Hi {{*first_name*}} - On behalf of everyone at

{{*company*}} I wanted to reach out and thank you for renewing your {{*contract/subscription*}} with

{{*product/service*}}.

We are thrilled to have you as a customer and are here to help support you in any way we can.

That said, I would love to get on a phone call to talk about how we can help achieve any upcoming goals you hope to achieve. Let me know when works best for you and I will schedule you on my calendar.

Looking forward to catching up,

{{*your_name*}}

Message - Customer Renewal 7:

Hi {{*first_name*}} - I am so glad you have renewed with your {*contract/subscription*}} with {{*product/service*}}. I love being able to support you and {{*company*}} in {{*goal*}}.

Is there anything I can do for you at this time? Always here to help if you need me,
{{*your_name*}}

Message - Customer Renewal 8:

Hi {{*first_name*}} - I am reaching out to personally thank you for renewing your {{*contract/ subscription*}} with {{*product/service*}}.

If you don't mind sharing your experience with the product thus far, I would greatly appreciate it!

Here is a link to our survey. In exchange, I'm happy to give you {{*gift*}} in exchange for the feedback.

Thank you in advance! Can't wait to continue exceeding your growth goals all-around,

{{*your_name*}}

Message - Customer Renewal 9:

Hi {{*first_name*}} - You've renewed your {{*contract/ subscription*}} with {{*product/service*}}! Congratulations!

Here's to another year of growth and success! We love having you as a customer and are here to help support you in any way we can.

Please let me know if there is anything I can do to help you {{*goal*}}.

Cheers!

{{*your_name*}}

Message - Customer Renewal 10:

Hi {{*first_name*}} - Thank you for renewing your {{*contract/subscription*}} with {{*product/service*}}! We truly value you as a customer and want to partner with you along the way to success.

What do you like most about {{*product/service*}} so far? How can we improve?

Your feedback is important to us. Very much looking forward to another {{*contract length*}} partnering together!

Best,

{{*your_name*}}

MESSAGE SCRIPTS, LOST CUSTOMER FOLLOW UP

Message
Lost Customer Follow Up 1:

Hi {{*first_name*}} - I wanted to reach out to see how things are going since {{*leaving/canceling*}} with us at {{*company*}} and if there is anything we can do that would restart the conversation of doing business together again.

We are always here to support your growth in any way we can. Please never hesitate to reach out if you need anything.

Wishing you the best!
{{*your_name*}}

Message
Lost Customer Follow Up 2:

Hi {{*first_name*}} - I wanted to reach out to see how things are going since {{*leaving/canceling*}} earlier this year. Would you mind telling me some honest reasons for discontinuing {{*product/service*}}?

I'm hoping we can find a solution to any problems we may not have been fully aware of.

I am always here to help and support your growth in any way I can. Please never hesitate to reach out if you need anything.

Best of luck,

{{*your_name*}}

Message
Lost Customer Follow Up 3:

Hi {{*first_name*}} - I hope this message finds you well. I'm reaching out to see how things are since {{*leaving/ canceling*}} with us at {{*company*}} and if we can help you in any way.

Have you found a new way to help you achieve {{*goal*}}? If so, I would love to learn more about that.

Hope to catch up soon,
{{*your_name*}}

Message
Lost Customer Follow Up 4:

Hi {{*first_name*}} - Hope your day is going well! I wanted to check in to see how you are doing since {{*leaving/ canceling*}} with us at {{*company*}} and if there is anything we can do to help you at this time.

I often check in with old customers to learn about how I could have done better, or what you may have found as a better alternative.

What is working the best and what do you find missing?

Let's catch up when your schedule permits. Here's a link to my calendar: {{*sender.calendar_url*}}

Talk soon!

{{*your_name*}}

Message
Lost Customer Follow Up 5:

Hi {{*first_name*}} - I hope this message finds you well! Earlier this year you {{*left/canceled*}} with us at {{*company*}}. I wanted to touch base to see how things are going and let you know we are always here to support your growth in any way we can.

What are some things we can do to re-start the conversation of doing business together?

We would love to get your feedback and assist you. Let me know how we can help.

Best,

{{*your_name*}}

Message
Lost Customer Follow Up 6:

Hi {{*first_name*}} - I am sending a quick message today to check in with you about how things are going since {{*leaving/canceling*}} with us at {{*company*}}.

We miss having you with us and want you to know we're always there to support your growth however possible.

Never hesitate to reach out!

All the Best,

{{*your_name*}}

Message
Lost Customer Follow Up 7:

Hi {{*first_name*}} - I wanted to send a quick message to make sure things are going well since {{*leaving/ canceling*}} with us at {{*company*}}.

I don't know if you've had time to find another solution to help overcome {{*pain 1*}}, but we've recently introduced {{*new feature*}} that might help.

If you're interested in learning more, you know where to find me. Otherwise, don't hesitate to reach out if you are ever in need.

Wishing you the best!

{{*your_name*}}

Message
Lost Customer Follow Up 8:

Hi {{*first_name*}} - How are things for you over at {{*company*}}? I wanted to reach out to you personally to see how things are going since {{*leaving/canceling*}} with us at {{*company*}}.

Is there something we can do to revisit the conversation and help leverage {{*solution*}} to overcome {{*pain 1*}}.

Let's brainstorm a few ideas and see how we can work together on this.

I am always here to support your growth in any way I can.

Have a great day,
{{*your_name*}}

Message
Lost Customer Follow Up 9:

Hi {{*first_name*}} - I hope you are well! I noticed your latest post. Looks like business is great!

I wanted to check in to see how things are going since {{*leaving/canceling*}} with us at {{*company*}} and if there is anything we can do for you at this time.

As one of our favorite past customers, we are always happy to help when you need us.

Wishing you the best!

{{*your_name*}}

Message
Lost Customer Follow Up 10:

Hi {{*first_name*}} - As promised, I'm checking in to make sure all is well with you over at {{*company*}} since {{*leaving/canceling*}} with us at {{*company*}}.

Have you thought more about how you might like to partner with us? I have a few good ideas if you are interested in getting back together. I'm free {{*days/ times*}}. How about you?

Have a wonderful {{*day*}},

{{*your_name*}}

MESSAGE SCRIPTS, NEW EMPLOYEE

Message - New Employee 1:

Hi {{*first_name*}} - So excited to have you on at {{*company*}}. We have been thoroughly impressed by you and can't wait to get you going.

Let me know if you need anything.

This year is going to be a big one!
{{*your_name*}}

Message - New Employee 2:

Hi {{*first_name*}} - We are honored to have you as your newest member of {{*company*}}. You are going to be a great addition to the team!

Let me know if you need anything.

Have a great day!

{{*your_name*}}

Message - New Employee 3:

Hi {{*first_name*}} - Welcome to {{*company*}}! We are so excited to have you and know you will fit in perfectly.

Let me know if you need anything as you start the onboarding process.

This year is going to be a big one!

{{*your_name*}}

Message - New Employee 4:

Hi {{*first_name*}} - Congrats on becoming the newest member of our team at {{*company*}}.

We are so excited to have you and impressed with your skill set and experience.

Let me know if you need anything.

Best of luck,

{{your_name}}

Message - New Employee 5:

Hi *{{first_name}}* - Welcome! Happy to have you at *{{company}}*.

Let me know if you need anything as you are getting started please don't hesitate to reach out.

I am here to support you every step of the way!

{{your_name}}

Message - New Employee 6:

Hi *{{first_name}}* - Thrilled to have you as part of the team at *{{company}}*! You are going to add a ton of value. I'm excited to see what you can do.

Let me know if you need anything.

Always here for you!

{{your_name}}

Message - New Employee 7:

Hi {{*first_name*}} - CONGRATULATIONS! So excited to have you as our newest {{*position*}} at {{*company*}}.

We have been so impressed by you and can't wait to have you as part of the team.

This year is going to be a big one!

{{*your_name*}}

Message - New Employee 8:

Hi {{*first_name*}} - I wanted to personally reach out to welcome you to {{*company*}}! We are so happy to have you on the team.

How does it feel?!

This year is going to be a big one!

{{*your_name*}}

Message - New Employee 9:

Hi {{*first_name*}} - Grateful to have you as a part of {{*company*}}. Can't wait to get you going.

Let me know if you need anything during these first couple of weeks. I'm happy to help you learn the ropes.

Congratulations! Excited to work alongside you.
{{*your_name*}}

Message - New Employee 10:

Hi {{*first_name*}} - I wanted to send a quick message to tell you how excited I am to have you as part of the team at {{*company*}}.

With you on our team, I'm excited to reach {{*growth goal*}} faster than ever before.

Let's make it an amazing year,
{{*your_name*}}

MESSAGE SCRIPTS, WEBINAR

Message - Webinar 1A:

Hey {{*first_name*}} - Hope you are well!

Curious, are you interested in leveraging {{*skills 1, 2, 3*}} on your social platforms?

If so, I have a great (and free) webinar I can send you a link to, along with {{*special offer*}}.

If you'd like to see how it works, just reply with the word "YES" and I can shoot you over a link to the webinar and message scripts.

And if you're not interested, no worries at all.

Cheers!

{{*your_name*}}

Message - Webinar 1B:

Hey {{*first_name*}} - Here's a link to the free webinar: {{*link*}}

*Note:** Once you register, on the confirmation page you'll get access to all the free {{*offer*}}.

Can't wait to hear your thoughts!

Cheers,

{{*your_name*}}

Message - Webinar 3A:

Hey {{*first_name*}} - Hope you are well!

If you are interested in building {{*skill 1, 2, 3*}}, I have a great (and free) webinar I can send you a link to along with some {{*examples of content involved*}}, etc.

Don't worry. It's not about being pushy, sales-y or spammy, but rather giving you the tools you need to succeed in {{*industry*}}.

If you'd like to see how it works, just reply with the word "YES" and I will send you the link to the material.

Thanks!

{{*your_name*}}

Message - Webinar 3B:

Hey {{*first_name*}}!

Here's the link to the free webinar: {{*link*}}

*Note: Once you register, on the confirmation page you'll get access to all the free {{*offer*}}.

Can't wait to hear your thoughts!

Thank you,

{{*your_name*}}

Message - Webinar 4A:

Hey {{*first_name*}} - I noticed your experience with {{*company*}} and thought you might be interested in building {{*skill 1, 2, 3*}}.

This free webinar I created teaches exactly that.

I can send you a link to it, along with some {{*examples of content involved*}}.

We already have {{*number*}} of people signed up and can tell this will be one of our most valuable webinars yet.

To see how it works, just reply with the word "YES" and I will send you the link to all the materials you need to begin. Cheers! {{*your_name*}}

Message - Webinar 4B:

Hey {{*first_name*}} - I'm excited for you to get started. Here's the link to the free webinar: {{*link*}}

*Note: Once you register, on the confirmation page you'll get access to all the free {{*offer*}}.

When you finish, please let me know your thoughts. Your feedback is super valuable!

Message - Webinar 5A:

Hey {{*first_name*}} - I am reaching out to others involved in {{*industry*}} who may also be interested in acquiring {{*skill 1, 2, 3*}}. I have a great (and free) webinar I can send you a link to, along with some {{*examples of content*}} we will be using.

Reply with the word "YES" and I will send you the link to the webinar and learning materials.

Have a great day!
{{*your_name*}}

Message - Webinar 5B:

Hey {{*first_name*}}!

Great! As I promised, here's the link to the free webinar: {{*link*}}

*Note: Once you register, on the confirmation page you'll get access to all the free {{*offer*}}.

I will see you soon!

Message - Webinar 6A:

Hi {{*first_name*}} - I have a new (and free) webinar for those interested in {{*skills 1, 2, 3*}}.

I can send you a link to it, along with all the details you need to get the most out of your time.

Don't worry, this is not about being pushy, sales-y or spammy, but rather equipping you with the tools you need to stand out in {{*industry*}}.

Reply with the word "YES" and I will send you the link to the webinar and message scripts.

Best,
{{*your_name*}}

Message - Webinar 6B:

Hey {{*first_name*}}!

Here's your free webinar! {{*link*}}

*Note:** Once you register, on the confirmation page you'll get access to all the free {{offer}} and I'll be there every step of the way, in case there are questions.

Can't wait to see you there!

Message - Webinar 7A:

Hi {{first_name}} - As a fellow {{position}}, I'd love to offer you this valuable (and free) webinar. It teaches you {{skill 1, 2, 3}}.

I'd love to send you a link, along with a detailed overview of what it all entails.

All you have to do is send me a quick "YES" and I will equip you with everything you need to get started.

Cheers!

{{your_name}}

Message - Webinar 7B:

Hey {{*first_name*}} - So excited for you to watch this free webinar!

{{*link*}}

By clicking the link, you'll get access to all the free {{*offer*}}. Shoot me a message to let me know what you think afterward!

Message - Webinar 8A:

Hi {{*first_name*}} - I stumbled across your profile, and based on your experience with {{*company*}}, I thought you'd enjoy a great (and free) webinar that teaches you {{*skill 1, 2, 3*}}.

Interested? I'll send you a link.

If it's not up your alley, perhaps you know someone else who cold benefit.

Send me a quick "YES" and I will send you the link. If someone else comes to mind, you can send it to them as well.

Looking forward to hearing from you,

{{*your_name*}}

Message - Webinar 8B:

Awesome, {{*first_name*}}

Here's all the info you need! {{*link*}}

When you get registered, you'll have access to {{*offer*}} right on the confirmation page.

When you have a chance, shoot me a note to let me know how it goes!

Good luck,

{{*your_name*}}

Message - Webinar 9A:

Hi {{*first_name*}} - I would love to send you a great (and free) webinar that teaches you {{*skill 1, 2, 3*}}. As a {{*position*}} for {{*company*}} I think it would really benefit you.

Does this pique any interest? If so, I can share the link. Simply send a quick YES, and I'll hook you up.

Cheers!

{{*your_name*}}

Message - Webinar 9B:

Hey {{*first_name*}}!

I'm pumped to have you involved... Here's the link:

{{*link*}}

Once you have completed registration, you'll have complete access to {{*offer*}}.

Can't wait to see what you think!

Have fun,

{{your_name}}

Message - Webinar 10A:

Hi *{{first_name}}* - Wow, you've got quite the expertise in *{{industry}}*. I'm sure you know that the industry is always changing and thought this free webinar we're offering could bring you one step ahead. In it, we will be going over *{{skill 1, 2, 3}}*.

Do you think you might find something like this valuable?

Send me a quick "YES" and I will get the link to the webinar over to you along with *{{materials}}* needed to get started.

Cheers!

{{your_name}}

Message - Webinar 10B:

Hey {{*first_name*}}!

Great to have you joining us.

Here's the link you'll need to get started: {{*link*}}

*__Note:__ Once you register, on the confirmation page you'll get access to all the free {{*offer*}}.

Please let me know how it goes and if you have any questions!

MESSAGE SCRIPTS, CONNECTION GROUPS

Message - Connection Groups 1:

Hi {{*first_name*}} - I just joined the {{*group-name*}}
and wanted to introduce myself to other experts in my
industry.

Thank you for all your contributions to this group and
appreciate the connection here.

Looking forward to playing a part.

Have an awesome week,

{{*your_name*}}

Message - Connection Groups 2:

Hi {{*first_name*}} - I just joined the {{*group-name*}} and wanted to connect with you here! Love what you're doing and I'm excited to join in on the conversations. Please let me know how we might be able to help each other!

Cheers,

{{*your_name*}}

Message - Connection Groups 3:

Hi {{*first_name*}} - I just joined the {{*group-name*}} and am connecting with other experts in the group like yourself.

What's been your favorite thing about this group so far?

Love what you're doing and I'm excited to join in on the conversations. Please let me know if there's ever any way I might be able to help.

Best,

{{*your_name*}}

Message - Connection Groups 4:

Hi {{*first_name*}} - I am really excited to be joining the {{*group-name*}}. I wanted to introduce myself and start building relationships with others inside the group.

I am so impressed with your experience and I look forward to getting to know you better.

Talk more soon,

{{*your_name*}}

Message - Connection Groups 5:

Hi {{*first_name*}} - I just joined the {{*group-name*}} earlier today and am so impressed with everyone involved.

I wanted to reach out personally and introduce myself. Looking forward to playing a part.

Cheers,

{{*your_name*}}

Message - Connection Groups 6:

Hi {{*first_name*}} - I am loving the {{*group-name*}} so far. Your comment today really caught my attention and I wanted to thank you personally for the insight about {{*topic*}}.

Thank you for all your contributions to this group and appreciate the connection here.

Looking forward to playing a part in that.

Enjoy your day,
{{*your_name*}}

Message - Connection Groups 7:

Hi {{*first_name*}} - Thanks for engaging with my post in the {{*group-name*}}. I wanted to reach out personally to introduce myself. It seems like we have a lot in common.

Thank you for all your contributions to this group and appreciate the connection here.

Looking forward to being involved.

Have a great one,

{{*your_name*}}

Message - Connection Groups 8:

Hi {{*first_name*}} - I believe I just saw that you joined {{*group-name*}}. Welcome!

It looks like we have quite a bit in common. I'm excited to be connected with and learn from someone like you.

Hope you have a great day!

Best,

{{*your_name*}}

Message - Connection Groups 9:

Hi {{*first_name*}} - I joined the {{*group_name*}} and wanted to reach out to introduce myself. Have you been part of this group for a long time? What can I expect? I'd love to hear your thoughts on it.

Cheers,

{{*your_name*}}

Message - Connection Groups 10:

Hi {{*first_name*}} - Thanks for adding me here on LI. I just joined the {{*group_name*}} and am excited to be connected with so many like-minded individuals.

I look forward to learning more about your {{*latest project*}} and about you!

Hope you have a great day!

Cheers,

{{*your_name*}}

MESSAGE SCRIPTS, EVENT PREP

Message - Event Prep 1:

Hi {{*first_name*}} - I noticed you will be attending the {{*event-name*}} coming up!

It looks like we're in similar industries and I wanted to connect with you ahead of time in case we have a chance to meet up.

Look forward to seeing what you think of the event and learning more about what you do!

Cheers,
{{*your_name*}}

Message - Event Prep 2:

Hi {{*first_name*}} - It looks like we're both attending the {{*event-name*}}!

I'm excited to meet up with like-minded people in the industry and thought I'd get a jump start and introduce myself.

We have a lot of similar connections and hopefully, we can meet while we're there.

Feel free to send me a message.

You can also email me here: {{*sender.email*}}. Looking forward to seeing you there!

{{*your_name*}}

Message - Event Prep 3:

Hi {{*first_name*}} - I noticed you might be going to {{*event-name*}} this year! Have you ever been?

It looks like we have similar connections and interests and thought it would be good for us to connect here.

What are you looking forward to most at the {{*event_ name*}}? Hope to see you there!

Cheers,

{{*your_name*}}

Message - Event Prep 4:

Hi {{*first_name*}} - Looks like you'll be attending {{*event-name*}} coming up! So will I. I'm really looking forward to it.

I wanted to connect with you ahead of time in case we have a chance to meet up.

Look forward to seeing what you think of the event and learning more about what you do!

Best,

{{*your_name*}}

Message - Event Prep 5:

Hi {{*first_name*}} - I am attending the {{*event_name*}} coming up and noticed you will be there as well! Small world.

I'd love to connect with you ahead of time in case we have a chance to meet up.

Excited for what's next!

Have a great day, {{*your_name*}}

Message - Event Prep 6:

Hi {{*first_name*}} - I noticed you will be attending the {{*event-name*}} coming up too! I can't wait for ____ .

Are you attending for anything specific?

I'd love to meet up with you while we're there if we get a chance.

Look forward to seeing what you think of the event and learning more about what you do!

Best,

{{*your_name*}}

Message - Event Prep 7:

Hi {{*first_name*}} - Looking forward to the {{*event-name*}} coming up! I'll be attending as well.

I'd love to meet up with you if we get the chance. It seems like we share quite a bit in common.

What's the best way to meet up with you there?

Cheers,

{{*your_name*}}

Message - Event Prep 8:

Hi {{*first_name*}} - I saw that you'll be attending the {{*event-name*}} coming up! Hopefully, I'll see you there.

It's going to be awesome!

Look forward to seeing what you think of the event and learning more about what you do!

Cheers,

{{*your_name*}}

Message - Event Prep 9:

Hi {{*first_name*}} - I'm glad you are going to {{*event-name*}}! I know we've been meaning to get together and this is the perfect excuse to finally make it happen.

Let me know what days/times will work best.

Looking forward to it, {{*your_name*}}

Message - Event Prep 10:

Hi {{*first_name*}} - I can't wait for {{*event-name*}}. I saw you will be speaking!

I will definitely be taking my entire team to listen in. Keep up the great work!

See you there,

{{*your_name*}}

MESSAGE SCRIPTS, POST EVENT

Message - Post Event 1:

Hi {{*first_name*}} - We met briefly at {{*event-name*}} this year and wanted to make sure we connected here.

I appreciate everything you do and hope you will reach out if there's anything I can do to help/ support you!

Stay in touch,

{{*your_name*}}

Message - Post Event 2:

Hi {{*first_name*}} - I hope you had an amazing time at the {{*event-name*}}. We loved every minute of it and of course, enjoyed meeting you (and your team).

What was your favorite part of the event for you? I loved it when... {{*personal.compliment*}}.

As always, let me know if there's ever any way I can help!

Stay in touch,

{{*your_name*}}

Message - Post Event 3:

Hi {{*first_name*}} - Wasn't the {{*event-name*}} last weekend amazing?! Jam-packed with valuable information.

So grateful we had the chance to meet and exchange information.

Keep me posted on your newest business updates and as always, let me know how I can help.

Cheers,

{{*your_name*}}

Message - Post Event 4:

Hi {{*first_name*}} - Great to meet you at the {{*event*}}. It's always so motivating connecting with like- minded industry leaders.

What was your biggest takeaway? Hopefully, we can stay in touch.

Thanks for connecting here and looking forward to seeing your posts.

Cheers,
{{*your_name*}}

Message - Post Event 5:

Hi {{*first_name*}} - I wanted to touch base after meeting at {{*event-name*}}. It was so great to talk to you about {{*topic*}}.

Good luck with {{*goal*}}.

Stay in touch,

{{*your_name*}}

Message - Post Event 6:

Hi {{*first_name*}} - So great to meet you at {{*event-name*}}. I am so impressed by your {{*project/ experience*}}.

Let's keep in touch and please don't hesitate to reach out if there's anything I can do to help/ support you! {{*your_name*}}

Message - Post Event 7:

Hi {{*first_name*}} - Loved running into you at

{{*event-name*}}! I had such a good time and learned a lot about {{*topic*}}.

Please reach out if there's anything I can do to help/ support you in {{*goal*}}!

Stay in touch,

{{*your_name*}}

Message - Post Event 8:

Hi {{*first_name*}} - It was such a pleasure to meet you at {{*event-name*}}. Thank you for taking the time to talk to me about {{*topic*}}.

Please let me know if there is ever anything I can do to help or support you!

Stay in touch,
{{*your_name*}}

Message - Post Event 9:

Hi {{*first_name*}} - I am so happy to have met you at the {{*event-name*}}. It's so fun to run into like- minded {{*industry*}} professionals.

I'd love to stay in touch here on LinkedIn. If there is ever anything I can do to help you with {{*goal*}}, please let me know!
{{*your_name*}}

Message - Post Event 10:

Hi {{*first_name*}} - I absolutely loved the {{*event- name*}}. I feel so blessed to have met you there.

I'd love to stay in touch here on LinkedIn.

If you see anyone in my network who could help you in any way, I'm more than happy to make an introduction!

Stay in touch,

{{*your_name*}}

MESSAGE SCRIPTS, TRAVEL OUTREACH

Message - Travel Outreach, To Someone You Already Know 1:

Hi {{*first_name*}} - It's been a while! I hope your business is flourishing and all is well!

I wanted to let you know I'll be in {{*city*}} soon for {{*event*}} and thought I'd see if you had some free time to get together and catch up.

Let me know if you will be in town and if you have availability on {{*dates*}}.

I should be free {{*dates*}}.

Hoping we can make something work! Let me know.

Cheers,

{{*your_name*}}

Message - Travel Outreach, To Someone You Already Know 2:

Hi {{*first_name*}} - How are you doing? How is business going?

I wanted to let you know I'll be in your area on {{*dates*}} and would love to grab a coffee or take you for lunch and catch up.

Send me an email at {{*sender.email*}} or give me a call at {{*number*}} so we can set something up.

Looking forward to seeing you,
{{*your_name*}}

Message - Travel Outreach, To Someone You Already Know 3:

Hi {{*first_name*}} - It's been a while since I checked in and I wanted to take a minute to ask how things are.

I'll be in {{*city*}} soon for {{*event*}} if we could find time to get together to talk about {{*goal*}}.

Let me know if you will be in town and if you have availability on {{*dates*}}.

I should be free {{*dates/times*}}.

Let me know what works best for you! Best,

{{*your_name*}}

Message - Travel Outreach, To Someone You Already Know 4:

Hi {{*first_name*}} - Hope business is booming as usual!

I'm reaching out because I'll be in {{*city*}} soon for {{*event*}} and would love to sit down and catch up.

Let me know if you will be in town and if you have availability on {{*dates*}}.

I should be free {{*dates*}}.

Would really enjoy seeing you! Let me know.

Cheers,

{{*your_name*}}

Message - Travel Outreach, To Someone You Already Know 5:

Hi {{*first_name*}} - Checking in! I'm sure your business is flourishing and I hope all is well in your world!

If you're around, I'll be in {{*city*}} soon for {{*event*}} and would love to meet up.

Let me know if you will be in town and if you have an availability on {{*dates*}}.

I should be free {{*times*}}.

Look forward to hearing from you.

Cheers,

{{*your_name*}}

Message - Travel Outreach, To Someone You Don't Know 1:

Hi {{*first_name*}} - I hope this message finds you well! I noticed we have very similar backgrounds and connections.

It just so happens I will be {{*traveling/moving/new*}} to your area on {{*date*}}.

I'd love the opportunity to get together for coffee and meet others in the industry and get acquainted with {{*location*}}.

Let me know if you might be open to getting together. Hope to chat more soon,

{{*sender.email*}}

{{*sender.phone_number*}}

Cheers,

{{*your_name*}}

Message - Travel Outreach, To Someone You Don't Know 2:

Hi {{*first_name*}} - I hope this connection finds you well! I noticed we have very similar backgrounds and connections.

I'm going to be in/at your {{*city/event/etc*}} on {{*date*}} and would love to get together with other like-minded people in my industry while I'm there.

Do you have any availability on {{*dates*}}? Looking forward to hearing from you!

Cheers,

{{*your_name*}}

Message - Travel Outreach, To Someone You Don't Know 3:

Hi {{*first_name*}} - I wanted to connect and reach out because it just so happens I will be {{*traveling/ moving/ new*}} to your area on {{*date*}}.

I'd love the opportunity to meet you in person, and get acquainted with {{*location*}}.

Let me know if you have some time to meet up. You can contact me more directly here:

{{*sender.email*}}

{{*sender.phone_number*}}

Look forward to hearing from you! Cheers,

{{*your_name*}}

Message - Travel Outreach, To Someone You Don't Know 4:

Hi {{*first_name*}} - I noticed we have very similar backgrounds and connections and it just so happens I will be {{*traveling/moving/new*}} to your area on {{*date*}}.

It would be so great to meet up with someone who knows both the industry and the area well.

Let me know if you are open to getting together.

It would really help me get started networking in a new community. In case you'd like to reach out directly, here's my information:

{{*sender.email*}}

{{*sender.phone_number*}}

I greatly appreciate it,
{{*your_name*}}

Message - Travel Outreach, To Someone You Don't Know 5:

Hi {{*first_name*}} - I came across your profile while researching {{*industry*}} professionals in {{*location*}}.

It just so happens I will be {{*traveling/moving/new*}} to your area on {{*date*}}.

Would you be open to getting together for coffee? I'd love to meet you in person and learn more about {{*city*}}.

Look forward to hearing from you. Have a great day!

{{*sender.email*}}

{{*sender.phone_number*}}

Cheers,

{{*your_name*}}

MESSAGE SCRIPTS, THANK YOU

Message - Thank You 1:

{{*first_name*}} - Thank you so much for reaching out! It was so great to hear from you. I always appreciate your time and messages.

Have a great day!

{{*your_name*}}

Message - Thank You 2:

{{*first_name*}} - Thank you so much for your message. It brightened my day.

Hope all is well!

{{*your_name*}}

Message - Thank You 3:

{{*first_name*}} - Thank you so much for connecting me with {{*referral*}}. Things are really going well. If you ever need anything, please let me know!

Have a great day!

{{*your_name*}}

Message - Thank You 4:

{{*first_name*}} - Thank you so much for attending {{*meeting/event/lunch*}}. It was so great to see you and to talk about {{*goal*}}. Let's keep in touch.

Have a great day!

{{*your_name*}}

Message - Thank You 5:

{{*first_name*}} - Thank you so much for going over my {{*proposal/presentation/idea*}}. I know how valuable your time is and it really meant a lot.

Let me know if there is ever anything I can do for you in return!

Have a great day!

{{*your_name*}}

Message - Thank You 6:

{{*first_name*}} - Thank you so much for spending time with me to talk about {{*goal*}}. Your insights were powerful! I really learned a lot.

If I can ever help you in any way, don't hesitate to reach out.

Enjoy your day,

{{*your_name*}}

Message - Thank You 7:

{{*first_name*}} - Thank you so much for sending {{*mutual. connection*}} to help out with {{*goal*}}.

We have made huge steps in the right direction. I really appreciate you thinking of us!

Please let me know if there is ever anything we can do for you. Have a great day! {{*your_name*}}

Message - Thank You 8:

{{*first_name*}} - Thank you so much for taking time out of your day to mentor me on {{*topic*}}. I cannot emphasize enough how much I admire and respect your perspective and experience.

That conversation was a game-changer for me. I'll never forget it.

Have a good one,

{{*your_name*}}

394   Sponsored by Seamless.AI, The World's Best Sales Leads. Join for Free at www.seamless.ai

Message - Thank You 9:

{{first_name}} - Thank you so much for getting in touch with me about *{{topic}}*. I wanted to follow up on our conversation and make sure I answered all your questions.

If there is anything else I can do, please let me know!

Have a great day!

{{your_name}}

Message - Thank You 10:

{{first_name}} - Thank you so much for taking the time to interview me yesterday. I really enjoyed myself and am so impressed by you, your team, and *{{company}}* as a whole.

I look forward to discussing future possibilities in further depth. Excited to make an impact.

Cheers,

{{your_name}}

MESSAGE SCRIPTS, GENERIC POST ENGAGEMENT

Message
Generic Post Engagement 1:

Hey {{*first_name*}}!

Just a shout to say thanks for all the love on my posts lately :) Hope life is treating you well!

Cheers,

{{*your_name*}}

Message
Generic Post Engagement 2:

Hi {{*first_name*}} - Thank you for engaging with my posts!

It's been a while so I thought I'd reach out and see how things were going.

Any way I can help you? As always, let me know if you need anything. Hope you have an awesome day!

Have a good one,

{{*your_name*}}

Message
Generic Post Engagement 3:

Hi {{*first_name*}} - Thanks for the love on my posts lately! What's been your favorite? Wanted to connect with you here so we can keep the conversation going.

Let's see how we can help each other.

In the meantime, hope you enjoy your week!

Best,

{{*your_name*}}

Message
Generic Post Engagement 4:

Hi {{*first_name*}} - Hey thank you for engaging with my post {{*link to post*}} today! We were hoping you would find it of value :)

Could you do us a HUGE favor and comment or tag someone you think might like it too?

We always love the feedback and connecting with new people!

Thanks for playing such a big part! Let us know how we can help you too.

Cheers,
{{*your_name*}}

Message
Generic Post Engagement 5:

Hi {{*first_name*}} - Thank you for the frequent engagement with my posts!

I wanted to make sure you knew how much it means to me. As always, let me know if you need anything.

Hope you have an awesome day! Cheers, {{*your_name*}}

Message
Generic Post Engagement 6:

Hi {{*first_name*}} - Wanted to personally reach out to thank you for always taking the time to like/ comment on my posts here on LI.

You're awesome!

As always, let me know if you need anything. Hope you have an awesome day!

Happy {{*today*}}, {{*your_name*}}

Message
Generic Post Engagement 7:

Hi {{*first_name*}} - Wow! Thank you for all the love on my recent posts.

I wanted to make sure you knew how much it means to me. I spend a lot of time creating

content so it's nice to know when it resonates with someone.

Please let me know if you ever need anything. Hope you have an awesome day!

Cheers,

{{*your_name*}}

Message
Generic Post Engagement 8:

Hi {{*first_name*}} - Thanks for pausing to engage with my posts here on LinkedIn.

I really appreciate the love and support from someone I look up to so much.

As always, let me know if you need anything.

Have a great day,

{{*your_name*}}

Message
Generic Post Engagement 9:

Hi {{*first_name*}} - I wanted to take a minute to let you know how grateful I am for the love you show on my posts here on LI. Thank you!

How can I return the favor?

Have an awesome week!

{{*your_name*}}

Message
Generic Post Engagement 10:

Hi {{*first_name*}} - I saw you engaged with my post earlier today here on LI. Thank you! It means a lot to me when people take the time to support my content.

What should my next piece be about? Maybe we can collaborate!

Let me know your thoughts, {{*your_name*}}

MESSAGE SCRIPTS, HAPPY BIRTHDAY

Message - Happy Birthday 1:

Hi {{*first_name*}} - Happy happy Birthday! I hope this next year is your biggest and best yet!.

Let me know if there is anything I can do to help. Cheers and enjoy your day!

Message - Happy Birthday 2:

Hi {{*first_name*}} - Happy Birthday! Wishing you a beautiful day full of love and happiness!

All the Best,

{{*your_name*}}

Message - Happy Birthday 3:

Hi {{*first_name*}} - Happy Birthday! Wishing you a great day and a great year ahead!!!!

My Best,
{{*your_name*}}

Message - Happy Birthday 4:

Hi {{*first_name*}} - I just wanted to personally reach out and say Happy Birthday! Thank you so much for everything you do every day!

It's time to let the celebration begin because today is your big day!!! Enjoy the festivities and the cake too!

Cheers to another year in the record books and a huge year ahead!
{{*your_name*}}

Message - Happy Birthday 5:

Hi {{*first_name*}} - I just wanted to wish you a happy, happy birthday!

I hope all of your dreams and wishes come true this next year. Nobody deserves it more than you!

Have an amazing celebration and an amazing year ahead!

- {{*your_name*}}

Message - Happy Birthday 6:

Hi {{*first_name*}} - I just wanted to wish you a happy, happy birthday! I hope today marks the beginning of the best year of your life!

Have a great day today. You deserve it!

Cheers,

{{*your_name*}}

Message - Happy Birthday 7:

Hi {{*first_name*}} - I just wanted to wish you a happy, happy birthday! Any big plans??

I hope this coming year is filled with all the happiness and joy!

All the Best,
{{*your_name*}}

Message - Happy Birthday 8:

Hi {{*first_name*}} - HAPPY BIRTHDAY!

Wishing you all the greatest things in life this next year!

Much love,
{{*your_name*}}

Message - Happy Birthday 9:

Hi {{*first_name*}} - Happy Birthday!!!

So happy to have you in my network and learn from you. Wishing you all the best today and this next year!

Best,

{{*your_name*}}

Message - Happy Birthday 10:

Hi {{*first_name*}} - Happy Birthday!!!

I'm glad we met and can't wait to see what wonderful things this year brings.

Warm wishes,

{{*your_name*}}

MESSAGE SCRIPTS, NEW YEAR

Message - New Year 1:

Hey {{*first_name*}} - I just wanted to say thank you for being a valued connection of mine this past year.

I hope the New Year brings a big year full of cheer and joy!

All the Best,
{{*your_name*}}

Message - New Year 2:

Hey {{*first_name*}} - I just wanted to say thank you for being a valued connection of mine and wishing you a very happy New Year!

My best always,
{{*your_name*}}

Message - New Year 3:

{{*first_name*}} - Happy New Year!!! Thank you for being such an amazing connection and for bringing the LI community so much value.

I hope this next year is the best year ever for you.

Cheers,
{{*your_name*}}

Message - New Year 4:

{{*first_name*}} - I just wanted to say thank you for being a valued connection here on LinkedIn and I hope this next year is your biggest and best year yet!

Happy New Year and all the best.
{{*your_name*}}

Message - New Year 5:

{{*first_name*}} - Another year is here!!! I just wanted to wish you a Happy New Year!

Our best to you from ours this next year!

{{*your_name*}}

Message - New Year 6:

{{*first_name*}} - I just wanted to wish you a Happy New Year!

May this next year bring you the world full of health, wealth, happiness, wisdom, prosperity, peace and joy.

All the Best,

{{*your_name*}}

Message - New Year 7:

{{*first_name*}} - Reaching out to wish you a very happy New Year! May each day of the new year bring happiness and prosperity to you. Thanks for being a valued LinkedIn Connection.

Cheers to the best year you've ever had,

{{*your_name*}}

Message - New Year 8:

Hey {{*first_name*}} - I have loved following your professional growth this last year.

May the New Year bring you the best this world has to offer!

Best,

{{*your_name*}}

Message - New Year 9:

Hey {{*first_name*}} - What an incredible year it has been! Happy {{*year*}}! Wishing you the very best.

Thrilled to support you in any way I can.

All the Best,

{{*your_name*}}

Message - New Year 10:

Hey {{*first_name*}} - Wishing you the happiest New Year ever!

If there is anything I can do to help further your goals in {{*year*}}, don't hesitate to ask!

Cheers to {{*year*}},

{{*your_name*}}

MESSAGE SCRIPTS, WORK ANNIVERSARY

Message - Work Anniversary 1:

Hi {{*first_name*}} - Congrats on your work anniversary! I hope this next year is your biggest and best yet!

Let me know if there is anything I can do to help.

Cheers, and enjoy your day!

{{*you_name*}}

Message - Work Anniversary 2:

Hi {{*first_name*}} - I saw you have a work anniversary and wanted to say congrats! I'm sure it's been a big year. Here's to an even bigger one on the horizon!!! Best, {{*you_name*}}

Message - Work Anniversary 3:

Happy work anniversary! Enjoy every moment!
Have a great day!

Cheers,
{{you_name}}

Message - Work Anniversary 4:

Hi {{first_name}} - I just wanted to say congrats on your work anniversary! I hope this next year brings you a lot of happiness.

Enjoy, well-deserved!
{{your_name}}

Message - Work Anniversary 5:

Hi {{first_name}} - It's your work anniversary today! Every milestone is fun to celebrate so I wanted to make sure you were soaking it all up.

Hope you have an awesome day, {{your_name}}

Message - Work Anniversary 6:

Hi {{*first_name*}} - I just saw it was your work anniversary today! How does it feel?! Wishing you the best in all you do today and in the future.

{{*your_name*}}

Message - Work Anniversary 7:

Hey {{*first_name*}} - I saw it was your work anniversary today. Just wanted to say thank you for everything you do and hope this next year brings joy, cheer, and happiness to you and yours! {{*your_name*}}

Message - Work Anniversary 8:

{{*first_name*}} - Happy work anniversary! What an accomplishment. Congratulations and have a great day!

Best wishes,

{{*your_name*}}

Message - Work Anniversary 9:

{{*first_name*}} - I noticed today is your {{*number*}} anniversary for {{*company*}}! Amazing! Hope you are all celebrating your hard work over there.

Congrats,

{{*your_name*}}

Message - Work Anniversary 10:

{{*first_name*}} - Happy work anniversary! What a cool thing to have made it {{*number*}} years! Way to go. Such a great example.

Hope you have the best day!

{{*your_name*}}

MESSAGE SCRIPTS, INFLUENCER OUTREACH

Message - Influencer Outreach 1:

{{*first_name*}} - Happy {{*today*}}! Hope you are doing great.

Your work and advice changed my life in sales and helped me maximize my potential. I am now on a mission to help others accomplish the same with {{*company name*}}.

I'd love to give you, your newsletter readers and your clients {{*offer*}} in exchange for feedback on our new {{*product*}}.

Here's a link to the demo: {{*link*}}

When signing up, just have everyone use referral code:

{{*code*}}

Look forward to helping you and your network create more opportunities, faster than ever before.

Cheers,

{{*your_name*}}

Message - Influencer Outreach 2:

I put together a list of top startup experts to give {{*offer*}} in exchange for feedback. I came across your profile and think you are perfect for this.

{{*company pitch*}}

This {{*product*}} is a revolutionary {{*description*}}. Demo video here: {{*link*}}

I'd love to give you and all of your portfolio companies {{*special promotion*}} in exchange for feedback - No credit card, no demo, no catch.

Look forward to hearing what you think about it.

Best,

{{*your_name*}}

Message - Influencer Outreach 3:

Hey {{*first_name*}} - I love what you're doing on {{*social platform*}} and would like to offer you {{*offer*}} in exchange for feedback.

After looking through your profile I know you are perfect for this.

{{*company pitch*}}

This {{*product*}} is a revolutionary {{*description*}}. Here's a demo video: {{*link*}}

Check it out and let me know what you think.

Cheers!

{{*your_name*}}

Message - Influencer Outreach 4:

Hey {{*first_name*}} - After looking through your profile I am so impressed by the way you {{*compliment*}}. I love what you're doing on {{*social platform*}} and would like to offer you {{*offer*}} in exchange for feedback.

{{*company pitch*}}

This {{*product*}} helps alleviate {{*pain 1, 2, 3*}}. I've got a demo video for you to check out: {{*link*}}

Send me a quick message after you've had a chance to look things over.

I'd love to hear your thoughts.

Thanks for the help!

{{*your_name*}}

Message - Influencer Outreach 5:

Hey {{*first_name*}} - I am so impressed with the way you {{*compliment*}}. I love what you're doing on {{*social platform*}} and would like to offer you {{*offer*}} in exchange for feedback.

{{*company pitch*}}

Plain and simple? We help you conduct in less than

{{*time*}} time. This {{*product*}} is a revolutionary {{*description*}}.

Proof is all here: {{*link*}}

Send me a quick message after you have the chance to take a look. Excited to see what you think!

Thanks!

{{*your_name*}}

Message - Influencer Outreach 6:

Hey {{*first_name*}} - I would like to offer you {{*offer*}} in exchange for feedback.

The way you {{*compliment*}} is unlike anything I've seen. Super impressive.

{{*company pitch*}}

This is good for you, because it gets rid of {{*pain 1, 2, 3*}}. Here's a quick demo for you: {{*link*}}

Send me a quick message after you've had a chance to look things over.

I'd love to hear your thoughts and get you involved.

Best,

{{*your_name*}}

Message - Influencer Outreach 7:

Hey {{*first_name*}} - I love what you're doing on {{*social platform*}. *The way you connect with your audience is second to none. I'd love to offer you* {{*offer*}} in exchange for feedback.

We help {{*company pitch*}} by {{*value proposition*}}.

I'd love to send you this free video to see what you think: {{*link*}}

Send me a quick message after you've had a chance to look things over.

Would love to have you involved.

Best,
{{*your_name*}}

Message - Influencer Outreach 8:

Hey {{*first_name*}} - I came across your profile and you are absolutely perfect for {{*offer*}}.

I love what you're doing on {{*social platform*}} *and would like to give you* {{*offer*}} in exchange for your personal feedback.

{{*company pitch*}}

Our mission is to {{*mission statement*}}.

I made a video for you to check out: {{*link*}}

Your feedback is highly valued. Let me know after you've had a chance to look it over!

Thank you so much,

{{*your_name*}}

Message - Influencer Outreach 9:

Hey {{*first_name*}} - Loved your latest post on {{*topic*}}. It really caught my attention. Because of your interest in {{*topic*}}, I would love to offer you {{*offer*}} in exchange for your personal feedback. It would be extremely valuable to me.

The link to our demo is here: {{*link*}} Would you be open to checking this out? Let me know what you think...

Thanks!

Best,

{{*your_name*}}

Message - Influencer Outreach 10:

Hey {{*first_name*}} - May I offer you {{*offer*}} in exchange for your personal feedback?

I can tell you are {{*compliment*}} and your perspective would be super valuable to us at

{{*company*}} as we pursue {{*goal*}}.

{{*company pitch*}}

This {{*product*}} is a revolutionary {{*description*}}.

Let's sync up after you've had a chance to look things over: {{*link*}} Would love to hear your thoughts!!

Thanks ahead of time,

{{*your_name*}}

MESSAGE SCRIPTS, VENTURE CAPITALIST OUTREACH

Message - VC Outreach 1:

Hi {{*first_name*}} - I'm putting together a list of top startup experts to give {{*offer*}} in exchange for feedback and think you are perfect for this.

{{*product description*}}

{{*demo video*}}

I'd love to extend this offer to you, no credit card, no catch. Sign up here using referral code: {{*code*}}

P.S. Out of respect for your valuable time and inbox, I promise to keep this to a one-time email

Message - VC Outreach 2:

Hi {{*first_name*}} - Happy {{*today*}}!

I have officially put together a list of top startup experts to give {{*offer*}} in exchange for feedback and think you would be perfect for it.

{{*product description*}}

{{*demo video*}}

I'd love to extend this offer to you, no credit card, no catch. Sign up here using referral code: {{*code*}}

P.S. Out of respect for your valuable time and inbox, I promise to keep this to a one-time email

Message - VC Outreach 3:

Hi {{*first_name*}} - I hope this finds you well. I have identified top startup experts to give {{*offer*}} in exchange for feedback and yours is feedback I would highly value and appreciate.

{{*product description*}}

{{*demo video*}}

I want to extend this offer to you, no credit card, no catch. Sign up here using referral code: {{*code*}}

P.S. This will be a one-time email out of respect for your valuable time.

Thank you very much!

{{*your_name*}}

Message - VC Outreach 4:

Hi {{*first_name*}} - I hope this finds you well. In exchange for your feedback, I have put together {{*offer*}} for you and your team. I would really love and appreciate your thoughts on {{*product/service*}}.

{{*product description*}}

{{*demo video*}}

I want to extend this offer to you, no credit card, no catch. Sign up here using referral code: {{*code*}}

Let me know what you think!

Thank you for your time, {{*your_name*}}

Message - VC Outreach 5:

Hi {{*first_name*}} - Thank you for your time today. Because you are a startup expert I respect, I am offering you {{*offer*}} in exchange for your personal feedback.

{{*product description*}}

{{*demo video*}}

I would love if you signed up here using referral code: {{*code*}}

What do you think? I would love to hear back after you've had a chance to give this a try.

I appreciate it!

{{*your_name*}}

LI Message - VC Outreach 6:

Hi {{*first_name*}} - I would love to give {{*offer*}} in exchange for your valuable feedback.

Your perception could really help us achieve {{*goal*}}, and in return for your time, I want to provide {{*product/ service offer*}} that will enable you to {{*benefit 1,2,3*}}

{{*product description*}}

{{*demo video*}}

Sign up here using referral code: {{*code*}}

P.S. Out of respect for your valuable time and inbox, I promise to keep this to a one-time email.

Thank you for your time,

{{*your_name*}}

Message - VC Outreach 7:

Hi {{*first_name*}} - I have been looking for top startup experts to give {{*offer*}} in exchange for feedback and because of your experience with {{*company/industry*}}, yours would mean a lot to me.

{{*product description*}}. I would love to know what you think.

{{*demo video*}}

Sign up here using referral code: {{*code*}}

After you've tried it, what's the best way to reconnect?

Thank you in advance,

{{*your_name*}}

Message - VC Outreach 8:

Hi {{*first_name*}} - I hope this finds you well. I have been following your updates and am very impressed to see how much {{*project*}} is taking off!

I am providing {{*industry*}} experts with {{*offer*}} in exchange for feedback.

I would love it if you would provide yours as your experience with {{*experience*}} is extensive.

{{*product description*}}

{{*demo video*}}

No credit card, no demo, no catch.

Sign up here using referral code: {{*code*}} I'd love to know what you think.

Talk to you soon,
{{*your_name*}}

Message - VC Outreach 9:

Hi {{*first_name*}} - I see you've been up to some big things since I've reached out last - really impressed by {{*growth*}}.

I'm sending one last email out to top {{[industry]}} experts giving {{*offer*}} in exchange for feedback, and would love to hear what you think.

Based on what you are doing at {{*company*}}, I believe it could really benefit you and your team.

In fact, clients such as {{*related clients*}}, have started using this {{*product*}}, and they've already seen {{*growth*}}!

{{*product description*}}

{{*demo video*}}

Try it out for free on me. Absolutely no strings attached. Sign up here using referral code: {{*code*}}

Let me know what you think, {{*your_name*}}

Message - VC Outreach 10:

Hi {{*first_name*}} - I hope this finds you well. I have been researching top startup experts to give {{*offer*}} in exchange for feedback and you are at the top of my list.

Your insight would really be valued and appreciated. I also know {{*product/service*}} can really go a long way for you and your team over at {{*company*}}.

{{*product description*}}

{{*demo video*}}

If this piques your interest, I'd love to send you this referral code to try for free: {{*code*}}

P.S. Out of respect for your valuable time and inbox, I promise to keep this to a one-time email

Thank you for your time,

{{*your_name*}}

MESSAGE SCRIPTS, UPSELL

Message - Upsell 1:

Hey {{*first_name*}} - Thank you for that awesome testimonial! We appreciate the kind words.

How do you like {{*product*}} so far? What do you love most? How can we improve?

I would love to set a time to chat with you and ensure you're getting the most value you possibly can.

Let me know when you have a moment to catch up. Talk to you soon!

Cheers,
{{*your_name*}}

Message - Upsell 2:

Hey {{*first_name*}} - Thank you for being a loyal customer to {{*company*}}. We are truly grateful for you!

Wanted to check in to see how you're liking the {{*product*}} so far and to let you know we're running an exclusive special for existing users: {{*offer*}}

Would you be interested in taking advantage of this?

This is limited time, so let me know ASAP so I can hook you up.

Thanks!

{{*your_name*}}

Message - Upsell 3:

Hey {{*first_name*}} - Wanted to make sure you knew we're running a special deal to a select group of our customers and you are one of them!

{{*offer*}}

Give me a call {{*sender.phone_number*}} or shoot me an email {{*sender. email*}}.

This is a limited time thing only.

Let me know how I can help! {{*your_name*}}

Message - Upsell 4:

Hey {{*first_name*}} - You are absolutely killing it lately! I can see your hard work is paying off!

I've got a few free resources we just released that you might be interested in: {{*link*}}

Have an awesome day. Keep crushing it! Best, {{*your_name*}}

Message - Upsell 5:

Hey {{*first_name*}} - Thank you for your long time relationship with {{*company*}}. We are so grateful to have done business with you for {{*time*}}.

I wanted to check in to see how you're liking the {{*product/service*}}. We are currently running an exclusive special for existing users that I think you would really enjoy.

{{*offer*}}.

This offer extends through the end of this month. Let me know when you have any questions.

Thank you,
{{*your_name*}}

Message - Upsell 6:

Hey {{*first_name*}} - Thank you for choosing

{{*company*}}. We are so grateful for your customer loyalty.

I wanted to check in to see how things have gone with {{*product/service*}}.

We are currently running an exclusive special for existing users that I think you would take what you're doing to the next level:

{{*offer*}}.

We are offering it through the end of this month. Let me know if you have any questions.

Cheers,

{{*your_name*}}

Message - Upsell 7:

Hey {{*first_name*}} - Thank you for being a part of the {{*company*}} family. We are so grateful to have you as a customer.

I wanted to touch base and to see how things have gone with {{*product/service*}} and also let you know about an exclusive special for existing users that I think you would really enjoy.

{{*offer*}}.

It will be offered through the end of this month.

I would love to get it all setup and running for you. Please don't hesitate to reach out.

Cheers,

{{*your_name*}}

Message - Upsell 8:

Hey {{*first_name*}} - Thank you so much for partnering with us at {{*company*}}. We are so grateful to have you as part of our extended family.

How is everything with {{*product/service*}}? If you need anything please feel free to reach out.

I also wanted to let you know that we are currently running an exclusive special for existing users that I think you would really enjoy.

{{*offer*}}.

We are offering it through {{*time*}}. Take a look, and let me know if it piques your interest at all!

Have a great day,

{{*your_name*}}

Message - Upsell 9:

Hey {{*first_name*}} - So good to have you as a part of {{*company*}}.

I wanted to send a quick message to see how things are going with {{*product/service*}}. I heard you had massive success this quarter! That's amazing...

If you need anything please feel free to reach out!

Just an FYI, we are running an exclusive special for existing users that I think you would really enjoy.

{{*offer*}}. - This ends {{*time*}}.

Considering all the potential we've seen in the

{{*industry*}} industry this year, it could add so much value to your goals.

Let me know what you think and I'll get you set up!

Cheers,

{{*your_name*}}

Message - Upsell 10:

Hey {{*first_name*}} - We have absolutely loved having you at {{*company*}}. Your case study has been used to showcase the value of this {{*product/ solution*}} so many times which is amazing.

How is everything else going thus far?

I wanted to let you know that we are currently running an exclusive special for existing users that I think you would really enjoy.

{{*offer*}}.

This is an exclusive, limited time offer.

If this looks like something you would like to add, let me know ASAP and I'll get you set up!

Cheers,

{{*your_name*}}

MESSAGE SCRIPTS, EMPLOYMENT

Message - Employment 1:

Hi {{*first_name*}} - I noticed you posted in search of {{*job opportunity*}} with your company.

I happen to have {{*experience*}} and I'm connecting to let you know I just submitted my resume through {{*website, LI, etc*}}.

I am impressed with {{*company*}} and am very interested in exploring further conversation.

Please let me know how I can help and when might be a good time to schedule a phone call.

Thank you again!

{{*your_name*}}

Message - Employment 2:

Hi {{*first_name*}} - Thank you for connecting with me!

I've been loving all your company updates and recently came across the {{*position*}}.

Are you still looking to fill this role? If so, I'd love to learn more. My background in {{*industry*}} looks like it could be a match.

Are you free for a brief phone call to discuss?

Thank you for keeping me in mind and hope to hear from you soon.

Have a great day,
{{*your_name*}}

Message - Employment 3:

Hi {{*first_name*}} - I hope this message finds you well!

I'm an ambitious {{*student/job title*}} searching for ways my skills can make a big impact on companies like yours.

If you're ever looking for someone to take {{*tasks*}} off your hands, I'm currently learning to master {{*expertise*}}, and feel I could add a lot of value.

Experience is the best way I can get my foot in the door and show someone what I can do.

Thank you for keeping me in mind and I wish you all the best of luck this year!

Thank you!

{{*your_name*}}

Message - Employment 4:

Thank you so much for the opportunity to meet and interview with you and your team!

I look forward to taking the next steps in your hiring process and am excited about the future possibilities!

Let's stay connected here on LinkedIn!

Cheers,

{{*your_name*}}

Message - Employment 5:

Hi {{*first_name*}} - Happy {{*today!*}}

I am a recent graduate of {{*university*}} and am looking for opportunities to work with companies like yours.

I would love to take {{*task*}} off your hands and feel I could add a lot of value.

I would love to set up a time to meet and talk about possibilities. I am completely open to any suggestions you may have and would love to get my foot in the door.

Thank you for keeping me in mind! I look forward to hearing from you!

Cheers,

{{*your_name*}}

Message - Employment 6:

Hi {{*first_name*}} - Thank you so much for reaching out.

I recently came across the {{*position*}} and would love to talk to you in more detail about the value I can provide you and your company.

Are you still looking to fill this role? If so, Let's set up a time to meet this week!

My background in {{*industry*}} looks like it could really add unique experience and perspective to your team.

I look forward to hearing from you!

Cheers,

{{*your_name*}}

Message - Employment 7:

Hi {{*first_name*}} - I recently came across your {{*job post*}} for {{*position*}}. I would love to connect with you this week to learn more and discuss the value I can provide you and your company.

I have {{*experience*}} and have also submitted my resume through {{*website, LI, etc*}}.

Please let me know the best way to set up an interview.

Thank you again!
{{*your_name*}}

Message - Employment 8:
The Interview

Hi {{*first_name*}} - Thank you so much for meeting with me. It was great getting to know you and an honor to learn more about the {{*company*}}.

I would love any and all feedback you have for me. What could I have done better?

Is there anything I can clarify or provide as you are making this decision?

Thank you again for your time. Looking forward to the future!

Thank you,

{{your_name}}

Message - Employment 9: The interview

I wanted to connect with you here to personally thank you for the opportunity to interview with your team!

I'm excited about the next steps and looking forward to hearing from you again.

Cheers,

{{your_name}}

Message - Employment 10: The interview

Hi {{*first_name*}} - Thank you for connecting with me. I thoroughly enjoyed getting to know you today and look forward to continuing learning about the company.

I appreciate any and all feedback based on the outcome. What did you like/dislike? What could I have done better? Are there any questions that you need answered?

Thank you again for your time and hoping I can add value to your team.

Thank you,

{{*your_name*}}

MESSAGE SCRIPTS, NEW CONNECTION TESTIMONIAL

Message – New Connection Testimonial 1:

Hi {{*first_name*}} - I am so happy we had the chance to meet and work together at {{*company*}}.

Your expertise and leadership have really had an impact on my life.

As I grow and develop, I'd love to gather testimonies from people I value most.

I would love it if you considered writing me a short paragraph on your experience working with me.

I'm generally looking for a testimony highlighting my skills in {{*account industry*}}.

Any way you could help would be very much appreciated!

{{your_name}}

Message - New Connection Testimonial 2:

Hi {{*first_name*}} - It's been so much fun working side by side and accomplishing such huge goals this year.

I would love to get a short testimonial of your experience working with me.

What was the best part of our partnership?

Just a short one or two sentences would be highly appreciated.

Let me know how I can return the same favor. I have nothing but great words to say!

Cheers,

{{your_name}}

Message - New Connection Testimonial 3:

Hi {{*first_name*}} - I noticed you recently signed up for {{*service/product*}}. Congratulations and welcome to the team!

We would love to service you the absolute best way we can. How are we doing so far?

Your story matters to us and we would love a short testimonial of how you are enjoying your experience so far!

We'd love to return the favor however we can.

Let us know how we can be of help!
{{*your_name*}}

Message - New Connection Testimonial 4:

Hi {{*first_name*}} - Thank you for all the love on our posts lately! I can tell you are working hard to have your most successful year ever.

What's the latest? How can we best help?

We would LOVE a testimonial from you to feature on our blog. What do you think?

Let me know and let's keep in touch!

Thanks for your constant support and wishing you the best every single day of the week.

Cheers,

{{*your_name*}}

Message - New Connection Testimonial 5:

Hi {{*first_name*}} - I really enjoyed working on {{*account*}} together! Can't wait for the year to come!

I would love it if you could write me a short testimonial - just a couple short sentences about our success on the project would be greatly appreciated.

Let me know how I can return the favor!

Cheers,

{{*your_name*}}

Message - New Connection Testimonial 6:

Hi {{*first_name*}} - Thank you for all the love on our posts lately! I can tell you are working hard to have your most successful year ever.

We would love a testimonial from you to feature on our blog.

Let me know what you think! You can keep it as long or as short as you want.

Thanks for your support and wishing you the best every single day of the week.

Cheers,

{{*your_name*}}

Message - New Connection Testimonial 7:

Hi {{*first_name*}} - I really enjoyed working on {{*project*}} together!

I learned a lot from you and am so grateful to have met.

I would love it if you could write me a short testimonial - just a couple short sentences about our success on the project would be greatly appreciated.

Let me know how I can return the favor!

Cheers,

{{*your_name*}}

Message - New Connection Testimonial 8:

Hi {{*first_name*}} - Thank you for always engaging with our content on {{*social platform*}}.

What's the latest? Please let us know how we can best support you in {{*goal*}}.

In return we would really love to feature you on our blog.

Would you mind writing a short testimonial on your experience with {{*product/service*}}?

We would really appreciate it.

Keep it as long or as short as you want. We can't wait to highlight you.

Thanks for your constant support and wishing you the best every single day of the week.

Cheers,

{{*your_name*}}

Message - New Connection Testimonial 9:

Hi {{*first_name*}} - It's been so much fun working with you! Thank you for your encouragement and support over the years.

I would love to get a short testimonial of your experience working with me.

Just a couple of sentences would be perfect.

Let me know if I can return the same favor. I have nothing but great things to say about you and would love to give my recommendation!

Cheers,
{{*your_name*}}

Message - New Connection Testimonial 10:

Hi {{*first_name*}} - Thank you for being such a big part of my professional growth during my time at {{*company*}}.

I wanted to reach out and ask if you'd write me a short testimonial of your experience working with me.

It would really mean the world to me. I am also more than happy to return the favor at any time! I have nothing but great things to say!

Cheers,

{{*your_name*}}

MESSAGE SCRIPTS, TESTIMONIAL + TEMPLATE

Message - Testimonial Template 1:

Hi {{*first_name*}} - I am reflecting on all we've accomplished together this year, and am super proud to call you a client of mine.

Would you mind writing me a short testimonial of our project together?

As always, let me know I can help you too!
{{*your_name*}}

P.S. I included a template to help save time. Feel free to use as much or as little as you like.

{{*first_name*}} - {{*referral_name*}} *and I have worked together for* {{*time*}} *on* {{*project*}}, *and were able to accomplish* {{*goal*}} *in* {{*time*}}.

Not only did {{referral_name}} help improve {{result}}, but he did it with {{unique feature}}.

I would refer {{person/product}} to anyone looking to reach {{goal}}.

Thanks so much! {{first_name}}

Message - Testimonial Template 2:

{{*first_name*}} - I hope this message finds you well. I wanted to reach out to ask a simple favor.

Would you mind writing a quick testimonial for me?

Nothing fancy, just a few sincere lines about our partnership.

I have provided a template below if it helps. Thank you so much! As always, I am here for you any day of the week!

{{*first_name*}} - {{*referral_name*}} *and I have worked together for {{time}} on {{project}}, and I'm very pleased to have accomplished {{goal}}.*

Not only did {{referral_name}} help {{case study}}, but he did it with {{unique feature}}.

I would refer {{person/product}} to anyone looking to reach {{goal}}.

{{first_name}}

Message - Testimonial Template 3:

Hi {{*first_name*}} - Here is a template I generally give to people who feel unsure about what to say. Feel free to use this as an outline and expand however you wish! Thank you in advance.

Cheers, {{*your_name*}}

(see below)

{{first_name}} - I have known {{your_name}} for ____ short years.

In those years, {{your_name}} has motivated me to ____ .

I've watched him/her go from _____ to _____ and produce results like {{results}}.

I want to refer {{your_name}} to you at this time, especially because you are looking to increase {{goal}}. They are your missing link.

{{first_name}}

Message - Testimonial Template 4:

Hi {{*first_name*}} - Thanks again for being so willing to write a testimonial about your experience with me and {{*company*}}.

Here is the template I generally give to people who want to make this quick and simple. Feel free to use this as an exact outline, or expand how you see fit. I appreciate you as always!

{{*your_name*}}

(template below)

{{*first_name*}} - *I have known* {{*your_name*}} *for*
_____ *years.*

In those years, {{*your_name*}} *has helped me to* _____ *.*

I've watched him/her produce results like {{*results*}}*. Which*
enabled me to _____ *.*

I would definitely recommend working alongside {{*your_*
name}} *especially if you are looking to achieve* {{*goal*}}*.*

{{*first_name*}}

Message - Testimonial Template 5:

Hi {{*first_name*}} - Thanks again for being so willing to
do this. Here is the template I generally give to people to
help make the process easy and free of any confusion.
Feel free to use this as an outline exactly, or expand how
you see fit.

Sending my best!
{{*your_name*}}

(template below)

{{*first_name*}} - I have worked alongside {{*your_name*}} for _____ years.

During this time, {{*your_name*}} has inspired me in _____ ways.

I've watched him/her achieve _____ . Which enabled the company to _____ .

I would definitely recommend working with {{*your_name*}}. They are a great addition to any

{{*industry*}} team.

{{*first_name*}}

Message - Testimonial Template 6:

Hi {{*first_name*}} - I wanted to provide you with a template to eliminate any possible confusion. Please feel free to use this as an outline and expand however you wish! Thank you again. I really appreciate all you do! {{*your_name*}}

(see below)

{{first_name}} - I have known {{your_name}} for

_____ *short years.*

In those years, {{your_name}} has motivated me to _____ .

I've watched him go from _____ to _____ and produce

results like {{results}}.

I would be doing you a disservice if I didn't refer {{your_name}} for {{position}}.

Especially while you are working towards {{goal}}.

{{first_name}}

Message - Testimonial Template 7:

Hi {{first_name}} - Again, I am so grateful for your willingness to help me with this. Below is a template I give to people so they don't ever have to wonder if they are providing the right information. Feel free to use this as an outline or build on it as you see fit!

You're the best! Let me know if I can return the favor. {{your_name}}

(see below)

{{first_name}} - I have known {{first_name}} for _____ years. It has been _____ .

In those years, {{first_name}} has motivated me to _____ . I have grown in {{growth area}} because of their influence and example.

I've watched him go from _____ to _____ and produce results like {{results}}.

If you are looking to increase {{goals}}, {{your_name}} is the perfect fit for the position.

{{first_name}}

Message - Testimonial Template 8:

Hi *{{first_name}}* - I wanted to offer you the option to use a template in case you don't feel like you know exactly what information to provide for the recommendation. Feel free to use this as an outline and expand however you wish! Thank you in advance.

Cheers,

{{your_name}}

(see below)

{{first_name}} - I have known {{your_name}} for _____ short years.

In those years, {{your_name}} has motivated me to _____ .

I've watched him/her go from _____ to _____ and produce results like {{results}}.

I definitely recommend {{your_name}} for {{position, work, etc.}}, especially if you are looking to achieve {{result}}.

{{first_name}}

Message - Testimonial Template 9:

Hi *{{first_name}}* - Here is a template in case you feel you'd like some guidance on what to write. Feel free to use this as an outline and expand however you wish! I am so appreciative of your willingness to do this. It goes further than you know!

Cheers, {{*your_name*}}

(see below)

{{*first_name*}} - *I have known* {{*your_name*}} *for* _____
years. In that time I have watched him/her _____ .

{{*your_name*}} *has motivated me to* _____ .

I've watched him/her go from _____ *to* _____ *and produce
results* {{*results*}}.

You definitely want {{*your_name*}} *to be a part of your
team, especially if you are looking to increase* {{*goal*}}.

{{*first_name*}}

Message - Testimonial Template 10:

Hi {{*first_name*}} - Thank you for being willing to write
this recommendation. It will really go a long way for
me as I progress professionally. I wanted to provide this
template for you to make it as seamless as possible.

Thanks again, {{*your_name*}}

(see below)

{{first_name}} - I have worked with {{your_name}} for

_____ years.

In those years, {{your_name}} has become

I've watched him/herVen go from _____ to _____ and
produce results like {{results}}.

I would be doing you a disservice if I did not recommend

{{your_name}} for {{position}}, especially if you are looking
to increase {{goal}}.

{{first_name}}

SALES OBJECTIONS

During your sales emails, you are going to come across the same sales objections every single day; "I'm Not Interested," "It's Too Expensive," "I'm Already Working With Someone," "I Need To Talk To My Boss," "Send Me More Information," "I'm Not the Right Person," "How Much Is It?," "I Don't Have Time," "I Need To Think About It," "What's Your Guarantee?", etc.

To build a multimillion-dollar software company, I knew that every person on my sales team needed to be fully prepared to overcome any sales objection you could encounter.

As we built Seamless.AI from the ground up, we not only wrote this book to help you perfect your sales email, but we also wrote the entire *Seven Figure Sales System* book series to help you overcome any objection you encounter along the way.

The *Seven Figure Sales System* contains thousands of word-for-word sales scripts we've used to overcome any objection, selling any product to anyone in any market, and generate millions in sales.

CONCLUSION

In this book, I shared over 400 pages of proven social selling scripts, strategies, and secrets that I have personally used to build multimillion-dollar companies. These scripts have generated over

$100 million in sales, built two multimillion-dollar startups, and helped me raise millions in venture capital funding.

I could have easily kept all of these sales strategies a secret. However, I recognize that your success is my success. I know that these sales scripts will change your life, just like they have for me and I want you to be even more successful than I could ever be.

I spent over a decade writing and using all of these sales scripts and strategies. I cannot emphasize enough the importance of becoming an expert at studying and applying everything you learn from this book. If you want to maximize sales, you need to become an expert at social selling and this playbook should have helped you do just that.

By having the world's best sales leads matched with the world's best social selling sales scripts, strategies, and secrets, your success in sales is truly limitless.

It is my personal mission to positively impact one billion people and help all of you win our Seven Figure Club Award at **www.presidentsclubaward.com.**

I wholeheartedly believe that if you take action today from everything you learned in this book you will maximize your revenue and generate millions in sales.

By now, you have learned as much as possible about prospecting and selling with social selling. It takes just one sales list to change your life forever. I promise that if you dedicate the time and put in the hard work to be successful, you will win in the game of sales.

You are just one list away from the life you want...
You are just one list away from the family you want...
You are just one list away from the sales you want...
Build your list and go sell to that list right now!

I became a multimillionaire in sales by leveraging all the battle-tested strategies in this book, and I hope you do too. Please reach out to me with stories about your success using everything you learned in this book and I look forward to shipping your Seven Figure President's Club Award. Don't forget to apply for your award at **www.presidentsclubaward.com.**

I can't wait to hear from you, reach out to me at
brandon@seamlessai.com

HISTORY & ACKNOWLEDGEMENTS

This book is a culmination of all the hard work, effort, time, capital, resources, and writing I've done throughout my 15-year sales and entrepreneurship career. This book was written in less than 30 days because these sales scripts and strategies were created, tested, and saved over a decade and a half. This book would also not be possible without all the people who have positively influenced, motivated, encouraged, coached, and supported me throughout my sales career. Below is a list of many of the people I would like to thank for my success. If I miss anyone on the list, trust me I am thinking of you and am forever grateful - my publishing team just told me this book is already too long as is!

Thank you all for helping me positively change the world for the better.

To the Seamless.AI Team:

This book would not have been possible without our amazing team at Seamless.AI.

Most teams will tell you that you're crazy for wanting to write a book instead of focusing all of your time and energy on building a software platform like Seamless.AI. My team, however, demanded that I write these books. They knew that the sales scripts, strategies, and secrets that helped us generate millions could help you too.

Our mission at Seamless.AI is to positively impact and empower one billion people by connecting them to opportunities faster than ever before. We believe you are one list away from the life you want, the family you want, the marriage you want, and the sales you want. By sharing these books with you, this book is directly aligned with accomplishing our mission to help you sell to that list faster than ever before.

As we build a revolutionary real-time search engine powered by artificial intelligence that finds perfect emails and phone numbers for everyone you need to sell to, we are helping over 100,000+ sales teams automate all of their manual list building, prospecting, CRM data entry, and appointment setting work. This has empowered salespeople, marketers, and entrepreneurs to globally maximize sales.

I want to personally thank every single member of the Seamless. AI team. Each of you has helped me to complete this book.

Thank you, Dana, Alicia, Mason, Phil, Mike, Kristen, Jake, the sales team, the dev team, the design team, the marketing team, and our support team. All of you shape this amazing company in your own unique way and have had a massive impact on my ability to make this book a reality.

I couldn't have done it without all of you.

To My Wife Danielle:

I first want to thank my wife Danielle and our family, The Wolf Pack. Danielle and I have been together since the launch of my first company in college and it has been one hell of a ride. We've been through many ups and downs. We've been both very rich and very poor. We go all-in always, in all ways and that takes a lot of guts and risk.

When you are an entrepreneur you sacrifice a lot to make your goals and dreams a reality. The amount of pain, suffering, and sacrifice that you have gone through to build a successful business that positively impacts one billion people is very difficult.

Not many women could withstand, motivate, and inspire me through the endless years of ups and downs the way Danielle has every day. She is truly a superwoman, and I am so grateful, humbled, and thankful to have her by my side. Danielle always believes in me, no matter how crazy my ideas get. Whether starting an online sales and marketing company for the gambling industry, building a mobile software company, moving to New York, ditching entrepreneurship to sell for Google and IBM, or taking our life savings and investing millions into building Seamless.AI, she has been at my side, ready to go every step of the way.

Danielle,

You have no idea how much you inspire and motivate me every day. I want to put it officially in writing how much I love you and appreciate you. I am forever grateful for everything you do to support me and help me to make the biggest impact that I can on this world.

I am so excited for what lies ahead in this incredible journey and seeing how many people we can positively impact along the way.

To My Father:

I want to thank my father David, who taught me that anything in life is possible if you can dream it, if you are willing to work your ass off and if you dedicate your life to learning how to sell. No matter the challenge that my family faced, my father always stayed positive and always found a solution no matter what. He taught me how to work hard no matter what and how to provide for my family. My father also taught me that nothing is given in this world and everything is earned. Whatever you want you need to earn it by getting up early and staying late and putting in the work. He never gave me handouts, he always made me earn every penny I ever made and I am forever grateful for that. He engrained an undeniable work ethic in me and taught me to never stop, no matter what.

I am where I am today because of his love, influence, and his example. Thank you, Dad. Your sales experience has changed my life and I am going to use everything you learned and taught me to change the world and help change the lives of a lot of people for the better.

IN LOVING MEMORY OF THOSE WE HAVE LOST; YOU ARE ALWAYS ON OUR MINDS, AND FOREVER IN OUR HEARTS.

To My Mother, Stephanie, Who We Lost to Alzheimer's Disease:

Many of you don't know, but when I was in college my mother was diagnosed with early-onset Alzheimer's disease. By the time I was 20, she couldn't even remember my name and as years passed, her memory was non-existent. She passed away shortly after the disease and this was devastating to my family both emotionally, financially, and spiritually.

Mom, this book is an achievement and head nod to you. Shit as I write this, I am shedding tears wishing you could have seen everything I've been able to accomplish. As a kid, I would always tell you about all the amazing things that I would accomplish one day when I grow up, and I know you never truly believed I would achieve any of them.

I know it's not because you didn't believe in me, but instead, out of protection from how terrible of an upbringing you had. The amount of damage and abuse your father and mother did unto you is disgusting. I hope no kid or human should ever have to go through what you had to endure. If your parents were alive (they are lucky they aren't), I'd get them into the ring and knock them out.

You did the best that you could do to bring us up as kids by yourself with Dad constantly traveling on the road… and for that, I am grateful.

I am also grateful that I got to experience a tougher childhood growing up with you under those conditions. The way you raised me with tough love helped turn me into the most resilient, tenacious, whatever-it-takes, nothing-will-ever-stop-me, person that I am today.

Additionally, I am so damn grateful for your Alzheimer's disease, despite losing you to the heavens above.

The first reason is that you taught me life is short. I got to learn this early on in life in college when you first got hit with the disease. That inspired me to always give it my all for my goals and dreams because tomorrow isn't promised. You taught me that life is short, so just take the risk, and if you fail who cares. Get back up and try again or try something new. Take the shot because there is nothing to lose and can all be taken away from you in an instant. This has helped me become fearless in working to accomplish my goals and everything I am striving to become a great contributor to this world.

The second reason I am grateful for losing you to Alzheimer's is that your Alzheimer's helped inspire Danielle and me to research all the causes of the deadliest diseases in the world. Although you may have lost your life to one of the most devastating diseases in the world... I think you saved my life throughout the process. You gave a life to give a life. You gave your life, so I can get one.

You helped me research and discover the truth about the disease after college and how the food we eat can kill us or fuel us. All that research we did when you had ALZ helped us discover that there are no cures for these diseases after you get them... however, you can avoid the deadliest diseases in the world like heart disease, ALZ, diabetes, cancer, etc by not eating the food that causes these diseases in the first place like meat, dairy, processed foods, etc.

I am a whole-food, plant-powered leader because of you, and I truly believe my entire life will be lived healthier and longer than ever before. You saved my life because of all these changes I've made with my diet and I love you for that sacrifice.

Dad, Ashley, and I are always thinking about you, and I hope you are resting peacefully in the heavens above. Love you always, Brandon.

To My Mother-In-Law, Janice, in Heaven

Janice, I always tell Danielle that you are an angel from above looking down on me and taking care of us all. Ever since I graduated from college, your husband Don, Danielle, and Kristen took me in as their own when my family was working and living out on the west coast.

Don and your kids are the greatest human beings in the world and I truly believe they are incredible because of the amazing person you helped each of them become.

I hate cancer and I hate the pain that Danielle, Kristen, and Don had to go through when you passed away. All three of them were devastated and still feel the pain to this day but I believe with loss, comes perseverance. They are working hard to change this world for the better and they couldn't have done it without you.

I also call you my angel from above for several reasons. The first reason is that Danielle is the best 5-star plant-powered vegan chef a husband can ever ask for. She always tells me she learned how to cook from you, so I owe you like a Trillion dollars for that! I eat like A KING every night and wish we could have cooked and eaten together. She also helps keep our personal life and the house affairs in 5-star condition too, all of which she also says she learned from you! I don't deserve your daughter but I will work hard to keep her happy and protected every day.

I heard you were a little entrepreneur working on so many amazing different businesses throughout your life. I know we would have had a lot of fun working on all types of crazy companies together.

I am grateful you get to see all of us from above working hard to positively impact a billion others with our company today.

Your gifts bear fruits to this day. I love you and we are always thinking of you.

To Our Investors:

I want to take the time to personally thank all of my investors for their help in making this book and our company a reality.

Today we would not be able to support 100,000 salespeople, marketers, entrepreneurs, recruiters, and companies globally if it wasn't for the group of investors that have invested in Seamless. AI, in me, and in this amazing team of incredible people.

To all who invested in me and the company, we will do whatever it takes to maximize the success of your investment, the success of our customers, and the success of this company.

I will do whatever it takes and always put in the work to not let you down.

Sales Authors:

I want to thank all of the other sales authors out there who have impacted me beyond measure. Each of you has virtually educated, mentored, and empowered me to maximize my sales success.

I am forever grateful for everything that all of you have taught me as a result of taking the time to write books of your own. I love learning from other sales experts in the industry and I'm so thankful that you took the time and energy to share your expertise and advice. I read hundreds of sales books in my early sales career and my success wouldn't be a reality without you sharing your sales wisdom with the world. I am so thankful for you.

To the Readers:

Thank you to all the salespeople, marketers, entrepreneurs, recruiters, and anyone else reading this book working hard to maximize your sales success. My mission in life is to positively impact a billion people and to help you connect to opportunities faster than ever before.

Without you taking the time to read this book, or investing in and using our sales software at Seamless.AI, we would never be able to accomplish this mission. This past decade I have poured my heart and soul into helping salespeople, marketers, entrepreneurs, and recruiters to maximize their sales success and will continue to do so for the rest of my life.

I am forever grateful to you for buying a copy of this book, taking the time to read it, learning from it, and for writing positive reviews on it. I can't wait to hear about your success stories at **www.presidentsclubaward.com**

This book is dedicated to all of its readers. May it help you reach your full potential and maximize your sales success every single day.

Thank you so much for believing in me and supporting my efforts.

PLEASE WRITE A REVIEW!

If this book helps you out in any way, please help me to help others by writing a review! **http://amzn.to/2XldjAA**

Everyone is searching for books to help them improve their lives for the better… and the first thing they search for is the reviews.

If this book has a lot of amazing reviews with great comments, they buy the book and read it. If it doesn't have any positive reviews with great comments, they don't buy the book and read it.

I know this book can positively impact and help so many people… if we can get your support to write a great review with your comments on Amazon!

Additionally, I would love to read your review and hear how the book has helped you.

I print out every book review and hang them on my office wall to read for inspiration throughout the day. Your great review helps me personally to validate all the hard work and thousands of hours invested in writing this book for you.

Thank you again for reading this book and all of your support, I am truly honored and grateful.

I look forward to helping you make this next year your biggest and best yet!

CONNECT WITH ME

Personal website: **www.brandonbornancin.com**

LinkedIn: **www.LinkedIn.com/in/brandonbornancin/**

YouTube: **Brandon Bornancin YouTube**

Instagram: **@brandonbornancinofficial**

Twitter: **@bbornancin**

Email: **brandon@seamlessai.com**

The World's Best Sales Leads

Find Emails and Phone Numbers For Anyone.